BRINGERS
OF THE DAWN

Teachings from the Pleiadians

BARBARA MARCINIAK

edited by
TERA THOMAS

BEAR & COMPANY
P U B L I S H I N G
SANTA FE, NEW MEXICO

D1010398

LIBRARY OF CONGRESS CATALOGING-IN-PUBLICATION DATA

Marciniak, Barbara, 1948-
    Bringers of the dawn : teachings from the Pleiadians / by
Barbara Marciniak.
        p.   cm.
    ISBN 0-939680-98-X
    1. Spirit writings. 2. Pleiades—Miscellanea. I. Title.
BF1290.M265 1992
133.9'3—dc20   92-12393
                                                      CIP

Bear & Company, Inc.
Santa Fe, NM 87504-2860

Cover illustration: Peter Everly
Cover and interior design: Marilyn Hager Biethan
Author photo: Marsha Presnell-Jennette
Editing: Gail Vivino
Typography: Marilyn Hager Biethan
Printed in the United States of America by R.R. Donnelley

1 3 5 7 9 8 6 4 2

BRINGERS
OF
THE DAWN

To the Family of Light

CONTENTS

ACKNOWLEDGMENTS

I offer thanks to my friends, relatives, and ancestors whose strength of purpose led me to my own. A special thanks to my sister Karen, for her deep love and dedication to me and the "P's."

A spectrum of the Pleiadian work has involved travel to many sacred sites and teaching at them as well as about them. Early on I was led to Toby and Teri Weiss, both of whom have provided adept assistance in supporting the Pleiadian experience during our myriad of power-site tours.

Barrie and Susie Konicov first recognized the energy and brought the P's to print in *Connecting Link* magazine as a result of our being in Athens, Greece, on the same trip. They also introduced me to Tera Thomas, friend, coauthor, and editor of *Bringers of the Dawn*. She has had her life rearranged by working on this book; I have great respect for her ability to commit and transform.

Tera, Karen, and the P's somehow schemed this book into being. Barbara Hand Clow eventually came along and recognized the vibration, and her impulses and enouragement are directly responsible for bringing this work to publication. Marsha Andreola generously provided her encyclopedic knowledge of the tapes, and Richard Rodgers offered his ongoing support.

I felt overwhelming awe for the infusion experience of Gerry Clow, as he shared his journey of the material and offered me thanks for the opportunity to midwife this baby into existence! Gail Vivino inserted her expertise and fine-tuning skills to bring the book to its final stages, along with Barbara Doern Drew, Amy Frost, and the other Bear & Company staff. Marilyn Hager Biethan added the finishing creative touch with her exquisite cover and book design. Cover artist Peter Everly worked through inspiration and suggestion to create an image of dawn in space, light coded to trigger the viewer with a deeper message.

I honor the courageous, those who are willing to redefine the very essence of existence and to carry that renegade spark into a new version of the game.

My deep love and thanks I give to the Pleiadian consciousness, my teachers and friends, for their loyalty and their undaunted sense of duty and love, which galvanizes within me an energetic formula of galactic elegance, the ideal made real. Peace, prosperity, and thanks to all.

FOREWORD

When Barbara Marciniak and I met in 1988, we had both just begun an exciting new phase of our lives: I had moved to Michigan to birth a new magazine, *Connecting Link*, with publishers Barrie and Susie Konicov, and Barbara was birthing the Pleiadian channelings. After years of working many and varied jobs while traveling, searching, and studying consciousness-expanding material, we had created for ourselves work that encompassed who we were and what we believed, and we were excited about it.

During the next two years, Barbara and I traveled to many expos, played a lot with the Pleiadian teachings, and generally had a great time with all of it. We talked about doing a book of the Pleiadian teachings but never really pushed it; the book would come when it was time.

The year 1990, the beginning of the "unnamed decade," came. *Connecting Link* was getting well established, and Barbara had made some three hundred tapes with the Pleiadians. I felt it was time for me to move back to New York, where I could continue to do the magazine on my computer as well as do more networking. I also felt it was time to do the book.

When I thought of "the book," I imagined that the Pleiadians would dictate it to me and that I would simply transcribe the tapes, edit the material, and there it would be. It would take no particular effort and very little time out of my pressing magazine schedule. So, in May, when Barbara and I sat down to do a "book channeling," I was quite surprised to hear the Pleiadians' idea of how to do the book.

The Pleiadians assured me that they would not dictate the book to me and that I would have to pull it together through my own process. I was intrigued. They said to me, "If this book was just given to you, you would be an employee. What effort would it be of yours? It is going to be a birthing of something for you, a birthing of process in yourself that is a whole new way of utilizing creativity."

Phew! "OK, so, how do I do this miraculous process?" I asked. "Where do I begin?"

They answered, "You are going to piece this together using your intuition only. This is not at all to be a logical-mind project. By using your intuition, you will be guided and tested to see if you can perform and complete a project without your logical mind knowing the steps that are coming next. It will be a tremendous exercise for you. It will lift you into a much higher place of consciousness, a higher place of order, and a higher place of trust. When it is completed and is very successful, you will say, 'I don't know how I did it. I have no idea.'

"The story will show that if you can clear people of their personal information, they can go cosmic. The process that you will be going through during the next few moons will be very intense for you. You will go through the process of an initiation yourself as you write it. You have some mastering to achieve in a few areas during the next six moons, and all of this is tied together."

They said that I was to listen to the tapes and transcribe only the pieces that I *felt* would go into the book. Barbara's sister, Karen, would intuit what tapes had good information on them and send them to me. Also, my friend Marsha would get impulses on which tapes needed to be included. Then it would be up to me to pick out the parts to use. I was instructed to use no order and not to even think how they would fit together. I could use a one- to five-word code and a bit of color on each page to categorize the information, and that was it.

I began to grasp the idea. My logical mind had one more question. I asked the Pleiadians, "Should we attempt to find a publisher before the book is completed, or at least announce that we are doing the book?"

The Pleiadians replied, "Ideally, yes, you will send out the announcement that you are beginning the book. The first time that you sit down to work on it, clear your desk top and have no clutter or disorganization around you. Have a clean space, with your crystal stones that will assist you. Then you can make a prayer of intention by saying, 'I am now announcing that I am beginning a book, and I am sending this announcement out to anyone who is a publisher and to anyone who is involved in bringing this data into publication for those whom it will serve best. It is my intention that the person to publish this book discover me and be brought to me, and I promise that I will be available for that recognition. I understand that I have very little to do with this. That part is not mine. I understand that I am to broadcast the announcement like I am sending out the birth announcement and that a response will be sent to me. In this I trust.' That is it; it will be brought to you.

"Remember that the process you will be going through is very much a part of the story, because you will discover something of yourself; then the story will be told in the terms that you put together. You will understand the importance of the book because you will have had an experience as you create for others a pathway into reality based upon juggling your reality and allowing different sentences and contexts to be juggled through you and made into a new order. Someone who did not trust would find this very difficult. Trusting is the absolute key. There is nothing else that you can turn to in this process. This is about commitment, and you are going to learn that you can commit to who you are, that you will not screw up, that you will always be provided for and that never will you be left without. It will always all work out according to your intentions.

"Your part in this is to intend what you want and to simply let the data flow. The book will make its own order as you learn about yourself during the process and as you code certain information. It will be mind blowing what you experience."

As I now read the words they said to me then, I get a whole different picture than I did at the time. I realize now that they mentioned several times that doing this book was going to be an initiation for me, that I would be tested, and that people would need to clear their personal information in order to go cosmic. Now I know what those words mean; at the time, I had no idea.

My personal issues started coming up big time. I didn't trust myself, I didn't love myself, and, in fact, I didn't really know who I was—I couldn't separate the real me from the facade. I began a series of deep-tissue bodywork sessions that brought up more stuff—memories from childhood that I'd blocked out, trauma and pain stored in my body. I was a mess. I was in no shape to work on the book, for I was barely managing to get the magazine out every two months as it was.

In October, I went to Egypt with the Pleiadians. I knew this trip was going to be an important turning point in my life, and I thought it would kick me into high gear so I could get to work and pump out the book. It was a wonderful trip, a powerful trip, and it flattened me like a board. It blew open my circuits and awakened areas in myself that I had no idea were there, many of them dark and ugly. When I got back to New York, I was definitely not capable of beginning the book and, in fact, I wasn't sure I would ever be able to do it.

The only thing I knew for sure at that time was that I had to move out of New York. I couldn't get centered or clear there and I felt bombarded with energy. I felt naked and exposed walking on the streets, and I couldn't use the subway anymore. It was time to get out.

That December, I moved to North Carolina. When something is right, it works out beautifully. Libby, one of the friends I met in Egypt, lived in a rural area south of Raleigh, and I knew I wanted to live there. I made an intention that I would have a house to move into before I came down there. I pictured what it would be like and what the land would look like, and Libby said she would keep her eyes and ears open. About a week before my move, my current landlord walked into Libby's shop and started complaining because her tenant was moving out with no notice. Libby said, "That's because it's Tera's house!"

I drove down from New York the following week with all my belongings and moved in. The house was just what I wanted—roomy, with lots of light, and on 175 acres of land. It was perfect! The minute I got there, I began healing. I lay on the ground or sat with my back to a tree and just let nature heal me. Healing myself was all I focused on.

In January, when I went to Michigan to typeset the thirteenth issue of *Connecting Link*, I realized that my time with the magazine was finished. I had grown a lot doing it, and now it was time for me to move on to something else—*what* something else I didn't know, but when I get these *knowings* I have to go with them.

When I came back home, I spent a few days asking myself if I'd been a total fool to give up a job when I now lived out in the middle of the country and didn't know where I would get another one. Then I realized it was perfect that I had no job: it was time to do the book. I began listening to the tapes and transcribing bits and pieces of them. The work went smoothly and easily, and things seemed to be flowing. I didn't question the order or attempt to make one. I just let everything flow through me.

During this time, the Pleiadians did a series of daytime classes for a few people in order to catapult us out of our issues. The classes were called "Firing Codes of Consciousness," and that's exactly what they did. I got to deeper levels of the issues I thought I'd finished with in New York. Those of us in the classes cleared much emotional baggage and developed a very tight bond with each other. The series ended with a rebirthing that was one of the most powerful experiences in my life.

I had another "book reading" with the Pleiadians in which they talked about the Bringers of the Dawn making the cosmic evolutionary leap in awareness possible by anchoring the frequency first inside of their own bodies. Suddenly, an awareness hit me: I hadn't been able to do the book in 1990 when we had first talked about it because I hadn't been able to hold the frequency yet; I hadn't been cleared out enough to do it. I asked the Pleiadians about this.

"You did not trust yourself, Miss Tera. You told everyone you did, but you did not really even like yourself. You compared yourself, and you were not honest with what was really going on with you, and people very close to you were mirroring this for you. You had to go deeper, as everyone must go deeper into the layers, for everyone has layers of self-hatred and dislike. You had to explore certain behaviors you had that did not work and discover the reasons for them, and that discovery brought you to be a Keeper of Frequency. This is why the book was given to you the way it was—because you had to have a major breakthrough in consciousness. By hashing over and translating much material that you would not even use, you went through a process of a direct relationship with us. You heard over and over again, in a neutral way, all of the things that you needed to directly apply to yourself if you did not wish to be left behind. And, you did it."

Then they told me that I had transcribed enough material and that the book was ready to be put together. I had no concept of how this could be done. Was I to read all of the pages at once and see where they fit together? I had some pages with only a few sentences on them and other lengthy excerpts of several pages. How was I to put it into some sort of order?

The Pleiadians said that every night when I was going to sleep I was to give them one minute and visualize the cover of *Bringers of the Dawn*. I was to play with this and change the artwork every night if I wished. I was just to look at the cover, open the book and begin reading the pages, and then go to sleep. The information would be shown to me in the dream state. They said I would begin to pull the book into existence by reading a book that already existed in the future. They said it would be no work for me—that they would do all the work. Well, why not?

The first week didn't go so well. I was doing the visualization before I went to sleep, but when I woke up I would panic looking at all the pages, and my logical mind would frantically attempt to read them all to make some sort of order. It was completely frustrating. Finally, one afternoon, as I was sitting in the middle of the floor in my office surrounded by papers and feeling about ready to cry, I said, "Hey, Pleiadians! You said you were going to do this work! I give up! Here, *you* do it!"

I started picking up the papers, one by one, like I was going to just stack them together and put them away. But I was picking up one from the left side, and then one from the right side, and then maybe one in back of me, and then one around to the left again. There was no rhyme or reason to this—no order to it. I wasn't even thinking about it, I was just picking them up. After gathering about thirty pages, I suddenly stopped and looked at the stack in my hand. I got chills all over, and I said to myself, "Oh my God, I think this is the first chapter." I took the pages to my desk, sat down and began reading. They fit together like a puzzle. I was shocked! I know I believe this stuff, but still, when it really begins happening it's quite amazing. The rest of the book began falling together effortlessly, to use a favorite Pleiadian word.

I had another "book reading" and told the Pleiadians how pleased I was with the new process and how much fun it was. They said, "It is the beginning of receiving direct guidance in how to do things. The more you say, 'I relinquish control, I don't know how to do this,' the more the energy will come in. As you get out of your own way, it will become easier and easier. All you need to do is intend. The more intending you do, the easier it will become. Later on, when the book is put together and many ask you how you did it, we want you to say that this is the process you used. We want you to verify our teachings as you were able to receive them by demonstrating that you believe what we are telling you.

"Remember how long it has taken you to grasp the process fully. We are not lecturing you—we are guiding you through this, pulling you back, reflecting back to you over and over again so that you can understand where the power of operation is. It is through clear intention—through acting as if, and then simply receiving continuously."

The rest of the book just fell into place, and, true to their word, the Pleiadians found us a publisher without Barbara or me doing anything. Of course, they hooked us up with Barbara Hand Clow—who better to understand how to get the material out to the public? And her excellent guidance brought me through a rewrite and a polish of the book that turned it from just another channeled book into something really wonderful. The Pleiadians were right. When I look at this book, I don't know how it happened. I didn't design it, plan it, conceive of it, or make an order of it. All I did was trust and allow them to work through me. It was a wonderful experience, and one that has changed my life. I have learned how to work with nonphysicals, and I will never again set out to work on any project alone. I'm writing an original screenplay right now, and I called in a group of experts to work with me on the writing and a group of experts to work on selling it. It's phenomenal how it's working out. It's truly effortless.

The Pleiadians thanked me for my work with them and my trust, and they said they wanted to compensate me and gift me with many paychecks from Spirit (paychecks from Spirit are not like normal paychecks that give one dollars and cents). They have gifted me with so many things. My most important gift from doing this book is myself. I now trust myself, love myself, and depend on myself, and I've opened my heart. Because of that new love of myself, I have drawn wonderful friends into my life who have become a family to me. I have healed relationships with my blood family, and I have drawn in a major surprise: twenty-four years ago I gave a daughter up for adoption, and she has found me. She lives only two hours away from me, and we are establishing a warm and close relationship. I'm thankful she is back in my life.

Another important gift has been confidence. I *said* I was a writer for years. I've even written for years. But not too long ago, I woke up one morning and was going over the pages of my screenplay that I'd written the night before, and I suddenly got this *knowing*—I am a writer! Not I'm *going to be* a writer—I *am* a writer!

Learning how to communicate with nonphysicals has been another priceless gift and has opened up many new areas to me. I'm beginning to communicate with animals, both domestic and wild. It's been a wonderful experience, and I realize that avenues of communication have been opened that I'm not even aware of yet. They are limitless.

There have been many, many other gifts. The Pleiadians told me that the process of this book would be the most powerful teaching of my life, and I agree. I'm thankful that I chose myself to do it, and I'm thankful for all the love and support I had from my family of friends during the process. And I'm very thankful to the Pleiadians for their love, their friendship, their encouragement, their support, and, most of all, for tricking me into my own evolution.

Tera Thomas
Pittsboro, North Carolina
March 1992

Tera Thomas was formerly editor of Connecting Link *magazine and is currently a freelance writer.*

PREFACE

Trapped in Bali! That's exactly how I felt, as I wondered why the bureaucratic necessity of an Australian visa had never been mentioned until now. With ticket and passport in hand and luggage on the scale, I was told I needed the document to board the flight bound for Darwin. My mind raced for the logic of the event and an immediate method to overrule it. I would will this one around! I was not new to this game and had been tested many times during the last four years on my ability to transform and transmute obstacles into messages and to move with the living symbols into a new vista of experience. Telexes were sent to the consulate in Sydney, and for the first hour's wait, I was certain I would be cleared, verified, and on my way to begin a Pleiadian teaching tour in the land down under. I had left North Carolina a week earlier, stopped in Hawaii for a brief visit, and now, after a three-day sojourn in Bali, was rested and ready to begin the next segment of a two-month odyssey.

I glanced at the terminal clock and noted the slow passage of minutes. I was patiently waiting for intentions and events to be set into motion. As time crept forward, its movement began a dawning within me that maybe, just maybe, I was not going to get on board. Perhaps this was going to be one of those times where, intend as I might, I was not going anywhere. I could feel my body resisting this new plan and the rearrangements that potentially would have to be made because I could not board the plane and meet my tour schedule. It felt ominous. Damn!

The eleven *p.m.* hour of departure had arrived, and with ticket, passport, and tour schedule, I was told to see the local Australian consulate on Tuesday, this being Saturday evening and Sunday and Monday being holidays. The next flight for

Darwin was scheduled for the day after I was to be there.

I surrendered, located a taxi, and, luggage aboard, headed for the retreat and solitude of the quaint seaside Balinese hotel I had left hours earlier. My room was waiting. I did not have an immediate solution to this potentially aggravating dilemma, and knowing that, I dropped it. I moved into the personal creation of comfort and trust that somehow this would all turn out fine and that if I was to be trapped anywhere, Bali was certainly ideal.

The next day, as I sat by the window of my treetop room, a second dawning brought the realization that I had committed to writing a preface for *Bringers of the Dawn* and that I was not going to move ahead into Australia until I was complete with that task! Sipping Balinese coffee, I was feeling nurtured by my surroundings and the lush vegetation that framed my view. I began to contemplate where to begin and how to insert into time and space myself and this phenomenal process called the Pleiadians that through me had created a life of its own.

As if haunted by a recurring dream, I have had the question put to me over and over again, how did it all begin? Early on I would respond by just delineating the impulses and sequence of events that had led to my actual channeling of the Pleiadians and stop there. Through the seemingly endless repetition of this question, however, an energy churned restlessly in my reality, and as I kept repeating the story, I began to get glimpses of a grander view, where events and beginnings came from many directions and multiple "times," to be woven, now, into a tapestry of purpose.

In childhood, I felt I was different and marked to stand out by inheriting an older brother who was mentally retarded. His presence offered many challenges to my young mind, and our family had many lessons to learn. It was only recently that I was impulsed by the P's, as I have affectionately come to call them, to reexamine old photos from childhood and to reconsider my interpretation of who I thought I was. Embracing this approach, this time I saw celestial-like love beaming from the face of my dear older brother, Donald, and in one photo after another the light seemed always to bend and illuminate him. I had not considered that I was, perhaps, blessed by his very presence.

Our family shared and explored its boundaries under the influence of my Polish maternal grandmother, Babci, who embodied a dignity and a pride that transcended her earthly experience. A pioneer and product of the vast European immigrations of the early 1900s, she was drawn to the land where, she was told, the streets were paved with gold. It was under her stabilizing influence that my two brothers, my first younger sister, and I played as children, exploring the magical land that was her domain. It was through her that I felt truly loved and learned to have great reverence for the land and for the love of Earth. She told us that her maiden name meant "Star" in Polish. Those teachings of loving the Earth would later be echoed through the voice of my own star connection, the Pleiadians.

In my teens, my so-called "difference" led me to an exploration of metaphysical ideas, and for the first time, I became excited with the discovery that there were many interpretations of reality from which to choose. By the late 1970s, I was exploring the Seth material among other things and thereafter spent a number of years recording my dream adventures while I absorbed page upon page of Seth lore.

In August of 1987—the summer of Harmonic Convergence—and again seven months later, in March of 1988, I experienced brief reality collapses, where segmented and stored events from a seemingly insignificant past came screaming forward, anxiously demanding a place of recognition. On these separate occasions, my body was catapulted into a state of shock, as data on UFO abductions was casually being viewed and shared by those around me. The first time this occurred, I somehow glossed over it, but the second time, my body was activated beyond anything I had ever experienced—or almost. Memories overwhelmed me. The presentation of the UFO data was tapping into my dream file, exposing a truth that was very difficult to assimilate.

Years before, in the early eighties, while living in Taos, New Mexico, I had had a late-night encounter in my bedroom with three bright-blue beings. At the time, the experience sent me into deep panic, not at all a common feeling for me. To resolve this conflict, for I had no frame of reference around which I could fathom my own relationship and safety to this unknown, I stored the event/experience in my Seth-inspired dream journals and left it there, an unexplained slice of reality that certainly wasn't a dream, though for years it would find a secure place in my psyche with that title.

Now the old question resurfaced. Under what category of life's files did my personal encounter reside? Was it really real? A replay of my encounter flashed into my now as every cell in my body suddenly knew extraterrestrials were real. My body would never forget the meeting of the three blue beings and how they hovered over me, calming me from some apparent, yet camouflaged trauma. My intellect was on call to expand its worldview—and comprehend. I was challenged to live with and integrate this experience, which would open me for what was to come.

The Pleiadians and I officially intersected realities a few months later in Athens, Greece, on May 18, 1988. I had been touring with a lively metaphysical group for almost three weeks through the temple sites of Egypt and Greece. Starting with the Great Pyramid, we moved through the ancient vortexes, innocent and naive as children, enthralled by the mystery stored within the silent stones. The trip concluded with visits to the Acropolis and Delphi, and as we were saying our good-byes in the hotel bar, something impulsed me with the notion to begin to channel by going to my room, sitting quietly, and imagining myself back in the King's Chamber of the Great Pyramid. I recall feeling inspired by this idea—I felt it was timely and in the spirit of the trip.

I proceeded to my room, and once I felt safe and secure, I sat with my spine erect and led myself with my mind back into the King's Chamber and the sound of many "om-ing" voices. To myself I said, I intend to become a clear channel *now*. Within a few short minutes I felt the urge to speak, and as this urge began to express itself in a whispered voice dissimiliar to my own, another portion of my mind—the rational, "in charge" version—began to question, through thought, the very voice that was speaking! This initial venture took great mental and psychic dexterity on my part—being that I was speaking for a heretofore unknown, directing questions in my mind to this unknown, and then listening to the answers so I could further direct the communication.

After what seemed to be a half hour, the unknown announced its presence as "the Pleiadians" and left it at that. The total communication was no longer than one hour. The "energies" had been distinct and abundant, and somehow I had been thrust into a rather blissful union of contact—the spoken words soothing me with answers—that today I can only recollect as feelings of wisdom and peace. Upon opening my eyes I was filled with a deep sense of wonder! Could this be? Had I stepped into something by following the deep-seated urgings that originally impulsed me to join this trip at the last minute, or had I dived too deep into the world of wishful illusion and dreamed it all up? What was the difference? And Pleiadians! I felt burdened by this from the start. Who in their right mind was going to believe I was in contact with and speaking for ETs? This was almost too much for my already long-established, quietly radical self to presume.

What inner turmoil my following all these impulses led to! I've since learned to trust and honor the energies that move me, and I can now read the tale of those initial impulses in my astrological birth chart and within the Pleiadian chart as well. During the first month of our relationship, the P's suggested that I begin to study astrology. Little did I know of the complexity and deep commitment to higher knowledge that this ancient science required in order to properly access a universal language and code of purpose. The Pleiadians, in their natal chart for that day of infusion, have a sun in Taurus at 27 degrees 57 minutes. The star cluster of the Pleiades is located at 28 degrees Taurus. Quite a trick indeed.

Back in the early stages of getting to know one another, I was not up on their tricks and the subtle methods they employed for notching my reality—I was too busy adjusting to the idea that I had contact with ETs. Our meeting and merging took practice to bring about greater ease, trust, and understanding. From the beginning, my sister Karen, who assisted me in the sessions, would eagerly await the appointed time when I would sit down to channel. She exhibited no doubts, but for myself, I kept wondering if this was really real.

In my desire to cooperate with what I had created, I *conditionally* offered the use of my body and my voice at appointed times, and I further stated that if the Pleiadians were really real, it would be no big thing for them to arrange things they wanted and do most of the work—my smug rationale being that I certainly wasn't going to waste my time with anything that was not a viable presence. This behavior may appear to be the height of absurdity to some, though those with experience in these realms understand that it is quite necessary to set boundaries. It took me a good two years to make a deep bond with them, and it came about during a body-therapy session, where a wave of Pleiadian love, like no other, engulfed me and imprinted in my emotional body the inestimable value they held for me. I surrendered.

Eventually I understood that the Pleiadians had demonstrated their subtle presence in my world from day one. They became the teachers and friends I had longed for. They seemed to have a direct line on the synchronicity/impulse game that brings people and events into being. Never having been a great investor in worry, it became quite easy for me to move into the Pleiadian moment of letting go, as they created a life of their own through me. People and opportunities came from every direction. My job was to manage and be a physical steward for their energies. All that they taught, I was to embody—to encounter and live.

Today we live in fine accord, and, truly, I feel more ET than human. They have made their teachings alive through me, and my life has become a Pleiadian mystery play, which has led me into the heartbeat of my multidimensional soul. Not that I claim to fully comprehend these encounters, and sometimes I wonder how so many people have gotten involved in my version of the illusion! I am deeply grateful for the opportunity to live a life freely expressed in these rapidly changing times, and for that creative expression to have birthed meaning in the lives of so many is, for me, a precious gift—the grace returned.

P.S. I did get to Darwin on time!

BRINGERS
OF
THE DAWN

ONE

Ambassadors Through Time

We are here. We are the Pleiadians, a collective of energy from the Pleiades. We have a long history. Our ancestors came from another universe that had achieved completion, a *universe.* You are simply working on a planet coming to completion, and we are here to help you with that task. This completion, or transformation, has been heralded by many for eons. It is an important time. What happens on Earth now will affect the entire universe.

Completion consists of you understanding who you are so that you can go further with the experiment. Our ancestors came from a universe that had completed itself and then understood universally that it was Prime Creator, the First Cause, or the journey of Prime Creator in time. They came from a universe that had discovered its essence—creativity. By discovering that essence, we found out that we are creators.

Our ancestors had a choice of returning to Prime Creator—which is simply movement—and being within that vibration, or of going on, as is always the case when completion of form has been attained. They chose to come into this universe as ambassadors because they realized that someday you would be ready for completion. They came into the Pleiades because that star system would someday be able to help you at the most difficult time, the crisis when you would be ready to reconnect with Prime Creator.

Our ancestors were some of the Original Planners of Earth, orchestrators who seeded worlds and civilizations with creativity and love. Because of their qualifications, they liked to orchestrate worlds just as conductors love to conduct. Our ancestors are also your ancestors, and we like to call you our ancient family, as indeed you are. Our ancestors gave their DNA to the Original Planners, and this DNA became part of the DNA of the human species.

We Pleiadians come from your future. In a version of our "now," there exists a place of tyranny and turmoil, and we have seen probable futures of Earth that include that same tyranny and decay. Time is greatly misunderstood in third-dimensional reality: you believe that time is measured in minutes or degrees. Time is much vaster than you realize. In actuality, time codes and plays with information, allowing you to move into realities simultaneously by stretching, distorting, curving, and twisting time around. You can get on an elliptical curve of time and experience many realities by simply going around the elliptical curve and discovering that, as time is not "solid," neither is reality.

As all realities are not solid, and as the future is not set (it is only a number of probabilities), we see an opportunity at this time to insert a more positive probability for Earth. We wish to reinsert light on this planet and restore Earth to its original purpose—that of becoming a magnificent intergalactic exchange center of information. So we have come back in a section of time to a place we call a kernel or a seed in order to effect change. This change will not only affect Earth, it will affect your future, our present, and the entire universe.

This is big news! You have come to Earth at a place and time when evolution is at hand. A major leap is about to take place that you came to participate in, and you are not alone, for many energies are coming to Earth now to participate in this great project. There are mother ships surrounding this planet that are acting as literal transducers of energy. There are beams of light coming to Earth from old and ancient star systems that have been working with you for eons. These beams of information are being blasted onto the planet.

As this information is being beamed to you, your body must be able to receive it, transduce it, house it, and beam it back out to others. Many of you will build telepathic links with these mother ships that will be like having your own radio stations through which you will be able to tune into a wealth of information at will.

This is the evolution of super-consciousness, the evolution into the highest aspect of your being. You do not need to worry about becoming this being, *for you already are this being,* and you just need to remember it. Since the veils around Earth were lifted at the time of Harmonic Convergence, you have been steadily beamed with this energy from the outer cosmos, and it is constantly being stepped up and increased as you are able to handle it. You are evolving now at such an extremely accelerated rate that each year of this decade will be like ten years or more from the previous century. Feel how much you will accomplish by 1999 and feel who you will be. It will be as if you have lived one hundred years in a decade.

You will be flooded with memory, flooded with many other things. Many of you will take trips upon the ships to various portions of the solar system. As you come into the Age of Light, worlds will open that you never knew existed. You have moved past the other ages: the Bronze Age, the Iron Age, the Industrial Age, the Information Age, and so on. These other ages had to do with seeding, planting, cultivating, and putting the potentialities of life into the third dimension.

A transition is about to occur, a dimensional shift that will lessen the density of the third dimension so that you will move into higher dimensions in which the body does not have such a solid state. You have come here because you wish to master the evolutionary process and be able to live with it. This is going to be very exciting, because it means that you are going to function in many realities.

Buried deep inside of you are all the answers. The questions that come to the forefronts of your minds are arising so that you can bring the answers from within your own beings. In order to achieve this, you must first *believe* that the information is stored there.

Humanity is learning a great lesson at this time. The lesson is, of course, to realize your godhood, your connectedness with Prime Creator and with all that exists. The lesson is to realize that *everything* is connected and that you are part of it all.

There are multitudes of cultures and societies that exist throughout the vastness of space, and these societies and cultures have been on and off this planet from the very beginning. It is not just that we, the Pleiadians, have come to assist; we are only one grouping from one star system. There are many who have journeyed here for many reasons. The majority of the extraterrestrials are here for your upliftment, though there are also those who are here for other reasons.

Your history moves in and out of very special times. Many of you became involved on Earth eons ago through star energy and through working with the higher realms. You know quite completely the difficulties that Earth has gone through, such as how many times the lands have shifted and how many times help has come from the skies.

Information was distorted when those who came from the skies to move you along in your development were turned into gods. As children idolize those who can do what they cannot do, your society clearly demonstrates this same method of creating godhood. The concept behind this method is one of the belief paradigms that you have come here to change. The third-dimensional world is one of great challenge, for it allows magnificent limitations to set themselves up. Through these limitations, structures are formed, and through this process, you create and learn that you are a portion of Prime Creator and that Prime Creator desires experience.

You are magnificent beings, members of the Family of Light, and you came to Earth at this time on assignment to create a shift, to make a change, to assist in the transition. Love is the key.

Love is what makes up the universe. The present technology on Earth will only develop to a certain extent because mankind does not yet understand that love is necessary. Energy can take all forms of creativity, but when one is dealing with greed or hatred or any emotion that is not working toward light, one is only allowed to go so far. There is only so much information that is available to that sort of vibration. Love is the basic building block, so when one has love, all possibilities exist. Bringing back the concepts of light, which are information and love—which is creativity—is the plan. It takes renegades like the Family of Light to come into a system that has been primarily dark for eons and change it.

We are very much renegades where we are. As we said, our own system is in need of transformation. We are working as a bridge or a link through the Family of Light in a variety of systems in order to change our own system. Your raising of consciousness through love and responsibility nourishes us, replenishes us, and expands our consciousness so that we may evolve further. Therefore, as we are friends and guides and assistants to you, so you assist us as well.

Where will this transition take you? We would like to see you become qualified to form worlds consciously. You are preparing to seed and be the species planted on many new worlds as they are being formulated, and because you have stored within your memories the history of what has occurred here on Earth, you will be able to teach others and consciously hold the direction in which other worlds need to go.

It is a vast plan you are participating in. All of you jumped at the chance to be here in such a challenging place at such a challenging time. You were certain you could do it. Also, you were told before you came here that there would be much assistance and that, at different junctures of your development, different entities would present themselves upon the planet in different capacities to trigger you, fire you up, and remind you—*not to do it for you*. We are one of those triggers, a catalyst. When you hear the name *Pleiadians*, you feel a connection because we are assisting you in bringing your own information, your own knowing, forward.

By working with you, it is our intention to offer you a reminder of who you are so that you can find the greatest source for your own inspiration. If we could assign a career to each of you or give you a way of being, we would ask each of you to become an inspiration. When you are able to live in this capacity and to be truly an inspiration to all who encounter you, you will be *living your light*, and that is quite profound.

Remember that we are here for our reasons and that you are here for your reasons and that we are all here to evolve together and create a new vibrational frequency. We wish to break belief paradigms that separate individuals as they evolve. We wish to create an ambassadorship, a game of harmony and cooperation, by giving you information that strikes you at the core of your beings, no matter what your former beliefs have been.

We, the group that speaks to you, are intending to fill our own resume with some interesting experiences. When we first began speaking in 1988, our collective consisted of fifty to seventy-five entities—some physical, some nonphysical, all Pleiadian. Our numbers have been growing, and our collective now consists of well over one hundred entities from many different systems. We can now be called Pleiadians Plus. There are those in our reality who do not believe that we can accomplish what we have set out to do with you. They feel that we are taking too many chances and too many risks, yet they are sitting on the edges of their seats to see what will happen.

There are those in your system who believe we are here to spread fear, but we do not see it that way. We do not wish to scare any of you: we simply wish to inform you. If you sit in a dark room and you hear strange sounds, it can be fearful. However, if you turn on the light to see what is making the sounds, it is then not so scary. We wish you to be informed about what you are dealing with. Light is information; ignorance is darkness. We want you to be working in the light, not in the dark.

We are involved in working with you because we wish to evolve our consciousness toward more free will and expression. Just as you are on assignment to change the system that you are within, we are on assignment to change the system that we are within. We are not without our purpose. As we said, we come from your future, and, in certain instances, we have our hands full. We need you, just as you need us. You, as members of the Family of Light, can institute, implement, or insert a grand new probability in the chain of realities that will implode in the next twenty years from this sector of existence because you physically live on this planet. It is *through you* that the transformation will occur. What you do now vastly affects us. What happens with Earth vastly affects us.

We are here to assist, to teach, and to evolve as we go through this process together. We give our version of things only to bring you into higher consciousness. We do not wish to say that this version, and only this version, is how it is! This whole teaching is designed with a great purpose in mind, and the stories that we tell you are set up to take you to a higher plane of consciousness. That is our intention.

The words that we choose and the concepts of which we speak are triggers for codes that are stored deep inside of your bodies. Your bodies are waiting for the questions to be posed so that you can begin to resonate with the answers inside of yourselves—so that the cellular memories within your bodies can begin to remember what they already know. As we speak to you, you will remember.

In speaking to you, we wish you to expand your definition of reality; however, never take anything we say literally. Always follow the larger spiral that we are intending to create that allows you to see the bigger picture. Never stop where we define an idea, since we are simply here to open up your paradigms and rattle your cages so that you can begin to find the activation of the real knowledge, the true knowledge, that is stored inside of you. That is where the data is, and we have come to awaken it in you.

We wish to throw out ideas for your consideration. We wish to encourage you not to get stuck on any one idea and also to embrace what you are hesitant about or are fearful of. Realize that when you face the so-called dark portions or shadow portions of yourself, you are creating an opportunity of liberation for all concerned. This comes back to the first and final tenet: *thought creates*. No matter what situation you find yourself in, it is the power of your thoughts that got you there. It is also the impeccable belief that thought creates that will transform your experience and the planetary existence.

We recommend that you do a little questioning of anyone who overdefines and tells you absolutes. It is important to hear many different opinions and many different stories. Listen to a person's story, then see if it feels right. Is it for your own benefit and upliftment? One of the things that we like to teach you is that it is up to you to decide what to do. We give you information; however, it is up to *you* decide what to do with it: *you* are in charge of your life, *we* are not.

We like to pride ourselves on being storytellers. There is a certain credibility and a certain sensationalism in the way we present data. However, a story that we tell you at one point is certainly not the only story; it is not the end, and it is never the only truth. It is only one fragmentation, one small portion of the bigger picture.

No matter what story we tell you today, we guarantee you that a year from now we will tell you a different story, because a year from now you will be able to comprehend things in a grander fashion. So the story will constantly evolve. Your task is to find your identity inside of the story, to find what you *know*—not what you want to believe or what you have been told. Trusting what you know is imperative, for knowing is your connection to Prime Creator. Each and every one of you is going to have to know that your life is about something as you begin to remember your role.

You yourself chose to be here. You are on assignment to bring memory forward and to bring the value of human existence back to the forefront of creation. *You are needed.* You have been in training for this assignment for lifetimes, and you did not come unprepared. All that you need to know now is inside of you, and it is your task to remember your training. This is not a lifetime when you are going to be taught new information. As we said before, this is the lifetime when you are going to remember what you already know, and we are just here to remind you of it. That is part of our assignment.

TWO

On Prime Creator's Journey

Humanity is an experiment. Humanity has been designed, as has just about everything else that exists within creation. Prime Creator began experimenting with creation a long time ago in this universe for the purpose of greater self-exploration, self-gratification, and self-expression. Prime Creator brought energies and essences of life—extensions of itself—into this universe and endowed those extensions with the gifts that it had. It gave willingly and freely of its capabilities. There are many other universes and many other ways of designing universes; this particular one was designed as a free-will zone in which *all would be allowed*.

Prime Creator said to these extensions of itself, "Go out and create and bring all things back to me." This was quite a simple assignment, was it not? In other words, Prime Creator was saying, "I am going to gift you of myself. You go out and gift of yourselves freely so that all you create in this universe can understand its essence as my identity."

These extensions of Prime Creator, which we will call creator gods, went out and began to experiment with Prime Creator's energy as it existed within themselves. They began to create their own hierarchy, which in turn created other hierarchies. Each succeeding hierarchy created another hierarchy to endow it with its own essence and to assist in the development of this universe. Eventually, in one of the galactic systems, a plan came together to design Earth as an intergalactic exchange center of information. It was an incredible plan. Earth was a beautiful place, located on the fringes of one of the galactic systems and easily reached from other galaxies. It was close to many way portals, the highways that exist for energies to travel throughout space.

There was much scurrying and shuffling to create individual representation from all of the galaxies here upon this planet. Some of the creator gods were master geneticists. They were able through their hierarchies to tie molecules together—encoded molecules of identity, frequency, and electrical charge—to create life. Many sentient civilizations gave of their DNA to have representation of their coding upon this planet. The master geneticists then designed various species, some human, some animal, by playing with the varieties of DNA that the sentient civilizations contributed to make Earth into this exchange center of information, this light center, this Living Library. The plan for Earth was a grand one.

The Original Planners of Earth were members of the Family of Light, beings who worked for and were associated with an aspect of consciousness called light. Light is information. The Family of Light created the information center they had conceived of; they designed a place where galaxies would contribute their information and where all would be able to participate and share their specific knowledge. Earth was to be a cosmic library, a place of incredible beauty that experimented with how information could be stored through frequencies and through the genetic process.

Outside the structure of time, 100,000 years can pass in what may be a year within the structure of time as you know it. These creator gods did not exist in time as you know it. A few hundred thousand years or a million years was nothing to them.

Different energies were brought into existence. There were species of humans on Earth perhaps 500,000 years ago who developed very highly evolved civilizations. We are not speaking of the civilizations that you call Lemuria or Atlantis; to us, those civilizations are modern. We are talking about civilizations that are ancient, civilizations that are buried under some of the ice caps of the far southern continent of Antarctica. The project of the Living Library on Earth was eventually fought over. It looked enticing enough to be owned by some. During Earth's early history, there were wars in space for ownership of this planet. Have you ever wondered who owns Earth? It's a prime hunk of real estate. Do you think it would go ownerless in space?

Skirmishes took place, and Earth became a place of duality. Certain creator gods who had the right to do whatever they wanted—because Earth is a free-will zone—came in and took over. We call this "raiding" the Earth. It was like corporate raiding on Wall Street. These creator gods raided Earth approximately 300,000 years ago–the time period, historically speaking, that you would call the beginning of human civilization. This is merely the time period that you, in this present day, are taught was the beginning of civilization. In actuality, it was only the beginning of the later phase, the phase of modern humanity.

When this skirmish occurred, a certain group of entities fought in space and won the territory of Earth. These new owners did not want the native Earth species—the humans—to be informed of what took place. Uninformed, the species would be easier to control. This is why light is information and darkness is lack of information. These entities beat out light, and Earth became their territory. It gives you a new idea of light, does it not? There was great radioactivity and nuclear action, and much of Earth was rent asunder. The original species, human creation, experienced great destruction and was scattered.

These new creator gods who were the new owners were also master geneticists. They understood how to create life, and they wanted this territory for their own reasons. Territories are created and held by certain energies for many reasons, one of which is that *there is consciousness within all things.*

Consciousness communicates continuously. Consciousness vibrates, or can be led to vibrate, at certain electromagnetic frequencies. Electromagnetic energies of consciousness can be influenced to vibrate in a certain way to create a source of food. Just as apples can be prepared and eaten in a variety of ways, consciousness can be prepared and ingested in a variety of ways.

Some entities, in the process of their own evolution, began to discover that as they created life and put consciousness into things through modulating the frequencies of forms of consciousness, they could feed themselves; they could keep themselves in charge. They began to figure out that this is how Prime Creator nourished itself. Prime Creator sends out others to create an electromagnetic frequency of consciousness as a food source for itself.

The new owners of this planet had a different appetite and different preferences than the former owners. They nourished themselves with chaos and fear. These things fed them, stimulated them, and kept them in power.

These new owners who came here 300,000 years ago are the magnificent beings spoken of in your Bible, in the Babylonian and Sumerian tablets, and in texts all over the world. They came to Earth and rearranged the native human species. They rearranged your DNA in order to have you broadcast within a certain limited frequency band whose frequency could feed them and keep them in power.

The original human was a magnificent being whose twelve strands of DNA were contributed by a variety of sentient civilizations. When the new owners came in, they worked in their laboratories and created versions of humans with a different DNA—the two-stranded, double-helix DNA. They took the original DNA of the human species and disassembled it. The original DNA pattern was left within the human cells, yet it was not functional; it was split apart, unplugged.

Within human cells are light-encoded filaments, fine gossamer threads of energy that carry information. When these gossamer threads are working together like a cable—the way fiber optics works—they form the helix of your DNA. When you were rearranged, you were left with the double helix. Anything that was unnecessary for survival and that would keep you informed was unplugged, leaving you with only a double helix that would lock you into controllable, operable frequencies.

A frequency fence, something like an electrical fence, was put around the planet to control how much the frequencies of humans could be modulated and changed. As the story goes, this frequency fence made it very difficult for the frequencies of light—information—to penetrate. When light frequencies *were* able to penetrate the control fence, there was no light to receive them. The humans' DNA was unplugged, the light-encoded filaments were no longer organized, so the creative cosmic rays that brought light did not have anything to plug into and hold onto.

What part do *you* play in this story? You are members of the Family of Light. The mere fact that you are reading this book shows that you are Family of Light. For some of you, this is just like a dream. We are reminding you of what you know inside yourselves. We have come onto this planet to trigger your memory banks—to inspire the human race through the band of light so that you will begin to remember who you are, to create your own reality, and to alter the frequency on the planet and claim rightful ownership of yourselves and this territory.

We, as Pleiadians, come back through time—into what would perhaps be called our past—in the vestige of representatives of light. We come back in order to share a frequency with you, a frequency that each one of you has agreed to carry on this planet in order to change the DNA of the rearranged human race. This is a big story. It could make headlines, you know.

The Original Planners are not about to lose the territory. Do you think they are going to give up so easily? The Original Planners began to call on the Family of Light to go in and infiltrate the project, to incarnate one-by-one and bring the light—as information via creative cosmic rays—into the place where it was lost. The Family of Light began its work here, coming into a system that was devoid of light and devoid of information. By mutating the laws of humanity, these creative cosmic rays began to pierce people's bodies, individual by individual, then group by group. In very small amounts throughout the eons were these frequencies of information brought onto this planet. At times, great battles were fought to keep out the light or information that was always looking to be expressed. The Original Planners knew that, cosmically speaking, this was a lesson for them in *allowing*, in understanding the creator gods who took their project.

The Original Planners set out to insert their own version of a plan to coincide with a time when the frequency of Earth would be altered, a time when the owners would perish if they could not change their own frequency. *Emotions are a source of food.* There are those whose food source is love, and the Original Planners intend to alter the frequency of Earth to that of love. The current owners' food source of fear, anxiety, chaos, hunger, and despondency must be removed.

Guess who is removing this food source? *You are!* As members of the Family of Light, you are renegades. You are systems busters, here to conquer your own fears and to show the rest of the planet that there is no reason to fear anything. You love to go in and cause trouble. You are famous, your branch of the Family of Light. You are famous for going into systems of reality and altering the frequency, thus bringing information. It is not your task as members of the Family of Light to proselytize. You simply go into systems and act as receptacles; you receive the creative cosmic rays into your bodies, the bodies that you occupy as humans. You are in disguise as humans, and you allow a process to take place.

You are coded, and as your memory begins to rise, you will respond to the plan with which you came here to participate to alter the frequencies. You will begin to hold, keep, and maintain a certain frequency and then to *live it*. Identity as frequency is the sum total of your physical, mental, emotional, and spiritual bodies broadcast as electronic pulsations. As you live your frequency, you affect everyone, every place you go. That is what you are doing now. There are many who already understand their assignment, and there are those whose memories are just beginning to rise.

The plan to change the frequency modulation affecting the human species entails the rebundling of your DNA and of the light-encoded filaments. The plan is gigantic at this time. Earth is assisting, in its own way, the evolution of the universe. Earth is where things are happening: it is the hot spot, the place to be. It is where the plan begins to blossom, and what happens on Earth is going to affect many, many worlds.

As members of the Family of Light, you agreed to come to Earth many times—in many guises and in many different time frames—to learn the ropes, to figure out the character, and to become trained. You needed to experience Earth and to prepare yourself for the time when the frequency alteration would begin to occur and you would all incarnate in large numbers to bring the plan into action.

The Family of Light everywhere is beginning to unite. You must all focus on what you have in common, not what you do not have in common. As members of the Family of Light, you bring information to the planet neutrally to stimulate your own growth. You need to do this—*for your own growth affects the growth of the planet.*

Your DNA will evolve from two helixes to twelve helixes. These twelve helixes correspond to energy centers, or chakras, inside and outside of your body. Millions of you on the planet at this time are on assignment, and you have agreed to carry the frequency to accomplish this. Handfuls of you are becoming impeccable, and these handfuls are affecting the others. Soon you will begin to have great clarity as to who you are and what your assignment is.

This process is an incredible evolutionary leap for one to be involved in, and it is going to take place on an accelerated path for the next twenty years. There are those who have already received a realignment of the twelve strands of DNA, the twelve helixes. These twelve spiral strands of DNA interact with one another in the body and outside of the body. The connection of the twelve strands means that the twelve energy or information centers can begin to function and send information back and forth to one another.

Traditionally, seven of these centers are located in the body, and five are located outside of the body. They are commonly known as your chakra centers and are aligned with the spinning of the twelve heavenly bodies that you know of at this time within your solar system—the twelve heavenly bodies that are vibrating, as you recognize them, in 3D. These twelve heavenly bodies are spinning with information: they spin with the chakra systems that go out to the end of the universe, and they spin with the DNA spinning inside your body.

When human DNA begins to rebundle as a twelve-stranded helix system and this information is acted upon, there will be incredible power. Individuals, simply by coming together and jointly intending what they want—jointly becoming a telepathic receptacle for energies from all over the cosmos—will change the face of the universe.

We call the rebundling process of your DNA a *mutation*. Once you, as members of the Family of Light, are able to take this mutation into your bodies, you will be able to integrate your twelve centers of information. You will begin to understand that *you create your experiences*, and you will learn to become *conscious creators*. More than that, you will become *conscious rememberers* of who you are.

As your tenth, eleventh, and twelfth chakras begin to open themselves, many off-planet energies will appear in your lives. These energies will occur on this planet as more and more of you hold the higher frequencies. The tenth chakra connects with the solar system, the eleventh with the galaxy, and the twelfth with a place in the universe. As you hold these frequencies, you will bring information onto the planet that will astound and shock most of the world.

There will be a merging of identities, a merging of cultures, an infusion of many "new world orders," and there will be much chaos and confusion. As members of the Family of Light, you can simply observe this, knowing that chaos and confusion must come to break down the system so that it can be rebuilt with light. As members of the Family of Light, you can understand that there is an evolutionary process taking place and that those who can handle the changing frequencies by all means will evolve. Earth is an exciting place to be at this time. It is a good plan, is it not?

THREE

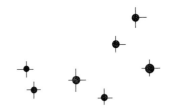

Who Your Gods Are

There are many misconceptions about the idea of godhood. The universes are full of intelligent beings who have, over time, evolved and developed all sorts of capabilities and functions to serve their needs to express themselves creatively. The importance behind existence and consciousness is creativity, and creativity takes many forms.

Eons ago, Earth was but a thought in the minds of great beings who had set before themselves the task of creating new forms of existence. Many of these beings affected the creation of this universe, and you have termed them *God*. In actuality, they were extraterrestrial light-bearing energies far removed from Prime Creator. We rarely use the term *God* with a big *G*. If we were to use that term, we would be referring to the entity we know as Prime Creator. Prime Creator, in its own personal implosion through love, endowed all things with consciousness. All things are Prime Creator on Prime Creator's journey.

We see ourselves as an extension of Prime Creator—always gathering information, going off on adventures, and doing whatever we need to do to make our lives more interesting and challenging so that we can feed Prime Creator. As we feed Prime Creator through our schemes and our endeavors, we endow Prime Creator with greater energy to give to new creations.

We have never gotten close to the entity Prime Creator. Even those of us who are beings of the grandest light vibration do not have the capacity at this stage of our evolution to be in proximity to Prime Creator. We are not prepared enough to handle the intensity of that emanation. It is our desire at some point in our evolution to get a glimpse of and perhaps merge with Prime Creator for a time. We know that this is possible, so it is something we strive for.

The evolution of consciousness and the ability to house information is what allows one to come into the proximity of Prime Creator. Many people on Earth have felt that they have merged with God. They may have merged with a *portion* of Prime Creator that best suited their vibration at the time. The total vibration of Prime Creator would destroy the physical vehicle in an instant, because it cannot house that much information. Those that represent "God" to you are but a minute portion of Prime Creator.

Even Prime Creator is but a portion of something larger. Prime Creator is always discovering that it is a child of another creation and that it is in a constant process of self-discovery and awareness. Remember, consciousness is within all things, and consciousness was never invented, it simply *was*. Consciousness is knowing, and your knowing is your closest place to Prime Creator. When you trust what you know, you are activating the God within you.

At this time, there is a great awareness moving over the planet as to how big the world really is and as to who's who in the world ballgame: not only who's who in the world ballgame, but who's who in the *cosmic* ballgame.

Just as you have hierarchies upon Earth that you may or may not be aware of, there are hierarchies in the cosmos. You can live within a certain area and not be aware that any hierarchy exists. You can farm your land, pay your taxes, decide not to vote, and simply be oblivious to any bureaucratic political structure. In somewhat the same way, Earth is oblivious to the bureaucratic political structure that operates in the universe.

It is important for you to understand that bureaucracies or hierarchies exist, and that these organizations have different experiences of time than you do. Others do not live within the structure of time as you know it. What you call one year perhaps to others may be only one small portion of a day. If you can really begin to comprehend this, you can understand why this planet has seemingly been left to itself for the last few thousand years. Now, activity is beginning to bubble and boil again from the skies, and you will be faced with inserting a vast amount of new knowledge into your paradigms and your belief systems. This planet is in for a culture shock—a big surprise.

You have come here at this time for a certain purpose: Those creator gods who rearranged the human species are returning. Some of them are already here. This planet has been visited over and over again, and many different forms of human being have been seeded here through a variety of experiments. There have been many influential factors that have created the course of history on Earth. There have been civilizations on this planet that have existed for millions of years that have come and gone and not left a trace. These civilizations, each and every one of them, were influenced by those you may term *God*.

Your history has been influenced by a number of light beings whom you have termed *God*. In the Bible, many of these beings have been combined to represent one being, when they were not one being at all, but a combination of very powerful, extraterrestrial light-being energies. They were indeed awesome energies from our perspective, and it is easy to understand why they were glorified and worshiped.

There is no literature on Earth that gives you a true picture of these beings. All of the gods came here to learn and to enhance their own development through working with creativity, consciousness, and energy. Some became very successful and mastered their own lessons, while some made quite devastating errors.

Who were these gods from ancient times? They were beings who were able to move reality and to command the spirits of nature to bend to their will. Humans have traditionally called beings *God* who could do things that the human race could not do.

These beings were passed down through the ancient cultures of many societies, portrayed as winged creatures and balls of light. The world is permeated with hints, clues, and artifacts of who your gods have been. However, those who wished to manipulate humans made up their own stories to create a paradigm that would control you. You were told that these beings were truly gods, and you were taught to worship, obey, and adore them. This paradigm is now on the verge of making a gigantic shift. The truth is going to come forward, a truth that will completely change the way you view the world. Woe be to those who are unwilling to look. The shock reverberations are going to move around the world.

The creator gods who have been ruling this planet have the ability to become physical, though mostly they exist in other dimensions. They keep Earth in a certain vibrational frequency while they create emotional trauma to nourish themselves. There are some beings who honor life before everything else, and there are also beings who do *not* honor life and do not understand their connection to it.

Consciousness feeds consciousness. It is hard for you to understand this concept because you feed yourself with food. The food for some beings is consciousness. All food contains consciousness at some point in its own development, whether you fry it, boil it, or pick it from the garden; you ingest it to keep yourself nourished. Your *emotions* are food for others. When you are controlled to bring about havoc and frenzy, you are creating a vibrational frequency that supports the existence of these others because that is how they are nourished.

There are those who live off the vibration of love, and that group would like to reestablish the food of love on this planet. They would like to turn this universe into the frequency of love so that it can have the opportunity to go out and seed other worlds.

You represent the renegade group of light, and you have agreed to come back on the planet. You are on assignment. You come into these physical bodies and take them over, and you intend, through the power of your spiritual identity, to change the physical body. You all selected with great care the genetic lines that would best give you head starts with all of this. Each of you chose a genetic history through which members of the Family of Light have threaded.

When human beings existed in their rightful domain and could understand many realities, they had the ability to be multidimensional, to be one and equal with the gods. You are beginning to awaken this identity within yourself.

The gods raided this reality. Just like corporate raiders in your time come in and take over a business because perhaps the pension funds are in great abundance, so the funds upon this planet were in great abundance at the time these raider gods appeared. In order to have you believe they were Gods with a big G, they rearranged you genetically.

That is when the Family of Light was scattered from the planet, and the dark team, which operated out of ignorance, came in. Your bodies carry a fear and a memory of striving for the knowledge that those gods represented and took away from you. The gods who did this are magnificent space creatures. They can do many kinds of manipulations and work with realities in many different ways. Humans, in ignorance, began to call these space creatures God with a big G.

God with a big G has never visited this planet as an entity. God with a big G is *in all things*. You have only dealt with gods with a little *g* who have wanted to be adored and to confuse you, and who have thought of Earth as a principality, a place that they own out in the galactic fringes of this free-will universe.

Before the raid, you had tremendous abilities. The original biogenetic example of the human was given incredible information, was interdimensional, and could do many things. When those creator gods raided, they found that the local species knew too much. The local species had abilities that were too much like those who were passing themselves off as God.

A biogenetic manipulation was done, and there was much destruction. There were experimental versions of the species brought onto the planet, where the original database was scattered but not destroyed. At one time, your DNA was intact. It was like a beautiful library where the information was all catalogued and referenced and you could find anything you wanted to find instantly. When the biogenetic alteration occurred to unplug the data, it was as if someone hid the reference system and pulled all the books off the shelves and heaped them into a pile on the floor so that there was no order to them. This is how your DNA was scattered and scrambled by the raiders a long time ago.

We are telling you a story now; there is definitely a story to this. We speak not to your logical mind but to your memory banks, so that you can begin to remember participating in this story. In this way, you will begin to understand what has happened and who you are within this process.

All of the genetic information was scattered; it did not have an order, but it was left inside the cells. The only information that remained for you to play with and to keep you functioning was the double helix. Many of the databases along the double helix were shut down, closed, so that you began to function with very little data. You were very easy to manipulate and control by many aspects of consciousness passing themselves off as God with a big G.

Certain entities took the existing species, which was indeed a glorious species, and retooled it for their own uses, their own needs. They disrupted the informational frequency inside human beings, changed the DNA, and gave you the double helix so that you could be kept in ignorance. Your frequency of accessibility was simply shut off so that you couldn't turn the dial of your own radio.

These creator gods set out to alter the DNA inside the human body, which is the intelligence, the blueprint, the code. If a code does not have a place to operate within, it cannot fire itself into existence or express itself into existence. If you are locked up in a little tiny room and never given any place to grow, you can never express yourself. The last number of thousand years, your code has been forced to fit inside a very limited DNA.

One of the most exciting aspects about being on Earth right now is that there is a reordering or a retooling taking place in your DNA. Cosmic rays are coming onto the planet so that a change is being broadcasted and a reordering is taking place inside the body. The scattered data that holds the history and awareness of the Living Library is now lining up.

The DNA is evolving. New helixes or strands are being formed as the light-encoded filaments are beginning to bundle themselves together. The scattered data is being pulled together in your body by electromagnetic energies from Prime Creator. We are here to watch this process in you, to assist you, and to evolve ourselves as well.

As this rebundling or reordering comes together, you will create a more evolved nervous system that will allow much more data to move itself into your consciousness. You will awaken many brain cells that have been lying dormant, and you will come into use of your full physical body rather than the small percentage that you have been functioning with.

Every place on the planet is being affected by this change, this awareness. Those of you who are the Guardians of Light and who wish to completely change this present reality and bring different options in are anchoring the frequency. If it is not anchored and understood, it can create chaos. It *will* create chaos. This is why you must ground yourselves.

Chaos brings about a state of reorganization when utilized properly. Time is collapsing, and the energy is becoming larger and larger. You have come here to use that energy first. You will make pathways of consciousness as you pull the energy into your body that will assist others so that they may not have to go through what you go through.

Many people will suddenly begin to feel this energy without any preparation at all. You are all pulling light, which is data and information, onto the planet, and as you do this you create new pathways for consciousness to explore without even saying a word.

The new pathways of consciousness create new realities, new options, and new ways of living and being. That is why the collapse of your society is inevitable: It does not hold light; it does not hold the multidimensional possibilities; it holds you in limitation, and you are tired of that.

The creator gods are space beings who have their own home in space. They are also evolving. There are those who would like to kick them out of the "creator god club" because they feel that they do not value the life that they create. Before the takeover about 300,000 years ago, many of the original team worked here to bring information and create this vast information center that was to be used to connect many galactic systems. Then there was a great war among the creator gods, and the space beings, whose stories are in the ancient manuscripts of this planet, won the fight. They came here because they wanted this place for many of their own reasons. In Prime Creator's universe here, *all things are allowed*. Because all things are allowed, many lessons are learned.

Some of these creator gods married and merged their lines, just as on the European continent different monarchs and royal families have married and merged their kingdoms. The creator gods would mix one kind with another to see what they could create. Remember, they understood genetics, and all things were created by manifesting and using the life force and understanding how the life force works. It is beyond your comprehension at this time how vast this project has been.

Who are these beings who came in and rent asunder the original plans for Earth? Who are these space beings we sometimes refer to as the Dark T-Shirts? Be kind when you speak of the forces of darkness. Do not speak as if they are bad. Simply understand that they are *uninformed*, and they create systems that are uninformed because that is how they believe they must operate. They fought at one time and separated *themselves* from knowledge, so now they desperately hold onto their existing knowledge and onto life as they have evolved it into being. It is life based on fear, life that does not honor other life, life that uses other life. Who are these beings? They are the reptiles.

These space beings are part human and part reptilian. We call them the Lizzies because we like to make things a little less emotional and a little humorous so that you don't take them so seriously and get so upset. We are not here to frighten you—we are here to inform you. You know all of this inside you, and as you begin to open the history of who you are, some of you will begin to access reptilian memories. You are under a delusion if you believe that you always incarnate as human beings. You incarnate to experience creation, to gather information about creation, and to comprehend it collectively. You certainly don't go into just one experience. It would be like eating dinner at the same restaurant your whole life and then saying, "I know all about food." It's foolishness. Begin to expand your boundaries and realize that you have to experience many things. There is brilliance within *all* life.

Creator gods take many forms, and they are not all Lizzies. There are creator gods who are insectlike. We Pleiadians are associated with the creator gods that are birdlike and reptilian. There were those who came from space and worked with the energy of the birds in many different cultures. If you look at the drawings of ancient cultures in Egypt, South America, and North America, you will see signs of the birds and reptiles. At one time, the birds and the reptiles worked together, and at other times they fought. As you comprehend more, the story will get larger. You will begin to remember your history.

The creator gods are very connected to you. When you decide to become a parent, you agree to learn from your children, to be responsible for their welfare, and to teach them to become responsible for themselves. It is the same with the creator gods. Through watching you grow, they are learning about life; they are learning about what they create; they are learning how to be good parents, so to speak.

Some creator gods created life just to have it take care of

them or meet their needs. They have fed off your emotions. One of the big secrets that has been kept from you as a species is the richness and wealth that accompanies emotion. You have been steered away from exploring emotion because through emotion you can figure things out. Your emotions connect you with the spiritual body. The spiritual body, of course, is nonphysical, existing on the multidimensional sphere.

The range of frequency modulation has now been shifted, and energies from the outside are working to alter the planet. These energies *need you*. They cannot alter the planet from the outside—the planet must be altered from the inside. The energies simply bring in creative cosmic rays that penetrate your body and create the evolutionary leap inside your body. Once you understand the proper use of emotion and begin to get control over your own frequency, you will be able to broadcast these rays. Then, you will not feed the frequency of fear to this plane of existence.

As the frequency of fear begins to diminish upon this planet, many activities will be promulgated to bring about an increase in fear because those who live off the fearful frequency will be losing their nourishment, their food. They will make an attempt to reinstate that frequency before they change their nourishment to the new frequency of love. The Lizzies have set Earth up with devices that can broadcast and magnify the emotional turmoil on this planet. That turmoil is sent to them, and it sustains them in some way.

In order to come to a planet, you must have a portal or way to get into it. You could fly into space, say to Jupiter, but if you never find the portal that allows you to enter the planet's time frame of existence, you could land on a place that looks desolate and without life. Portals allow you to enter the dimension of the planet where life exists. Portals open onto the corridors of time and serve as zones of multidimensional experience.

There have been different portals on Earth that have allowed different species, creator gods from space, to insert themselves. One of the huge portals that presently is being fought over is the portal of the Middle East. If you think back over the history of Earth, you will recognize how many dramas of religion and civilization have been introduced in that portal. It's a huge portal—with a radius of a thousand miles or so. This is why there is so much activity in the Middle East. This is the portal that the Lizzies use.

To some extent, the Lizzies have controlled this portal. They have used this area to create their underground bases and caverns, from which they operate. The ancient civilization of Mesopotamia, between the Tigris and Euphrates rivers, was a space colony where a certain civilization was introduced. Kuwait sits at the mouth of this territory. This is a portal that involves manipulation of the human population to serve the needs of others.

Within the Lizzie population, there are those who are benevolent and those who are malevolent. Why are we telling you all this? Why do you need to know it? You need to know it because the Lizzie reality is reentering and merging with your dimension. Part of your evolutionary leap in consciousness is not simply to go into love and light and eat ice cream sundaes every day. You must comprehend how complex reality is, how many different forms of reality there are, and how *they are all you*. You must make peace with them and merge with them to create an implosion of the collection of your soul. In this way, you can come back to Prime Creator.

You are going to be faced with many opportunities to judge many things and label them as bad. But, when you judge and label, you will not experience and feel the new realities. Always remember that this is a free-will zone and that there is a Divine Plan, which is going to be the last plan, the last card to be played. You all must remember that this last card is going to be an ace.

The nature of the drama on this planet is quite interesting. Whenever there is a frequency modulation of an existing system, there is a certain magnetism that moves out from that system. This magnetism draws every energy that was ever involved with that system back to the system so that it can be part of the evolution or process. You are magnetizing everything to yourself that you have ever experienced so that you can feel everything you need to feel about it.

The creator gods of ancient times are being drawn back here at this time because of the Divine Plan. They *must* participate in it and understand that their frequencies are going to be changed. They are resisting this, just like many humans are resisting. Yet, they create their own realities. These creator gods of the last 300,000 years have forgotten *who created them!* They have forgotten *their* gods.

As members of the Family of Light, you have not forgotten. Your task is *comprehension*: to pull comprehension and understanding onto the planet, which will stabilize the energy and generate the power to create. Light is underestimated on this planet, and these creator gods underestimate you. Even in their own brilliance, they have blind spots. They are so enamored of power that they fight amongst themselves.

The creator gods gave up a portion of themselves and became ensconced, enamored with their own project. You are linked to these beings because you are extensions or operable forces of them. You are here to affect reality not simply from the outside but from the inside. It is this that you are intending to remember.

The creator gods are coming back to raid you again because they don't want to starve. They understand that there is "systems busting" going on through you, so they are here to create greater havoc and fear, to fight once again for this territory. Their food source is important to them. They are losing control of the planet, so they are going back to their prime portal in the Middle East, where their nest is located underneath the ground, to create fear and chaos.

The Original Planners wish to bring freedom of choice with respect to frequency back to this planet. The gods who have been in charge here for this last period of evolution use frequency modulation and do not allow freedom of choice . They rob your psychic energy by giving you a false picture of reality in every way that you could possibly imagine. We are not saying these gods are bad. We are simply informing you of events that take place and of how innocently you become involved in these events. You do not realize that these situations are setups to get you to think or feel a certain way and to vibrate with a certain consciousness.

We play the same game. If you look back to see what we have done, have we not purposely set up a plan of frequency modulation for you? Have we not entrapped you, enticed you, con-vinced you of your free will so that you could choose to vibrate at a certain frequency? We have done the same thing the builders have done.

You had best, all of you, give up your old definitions of Santa Claus. In the same way that you discovered the truth about the Easter Bunny and Santa Claus and the Tooth Fairy, you are going to discover that there is a cover-up, a story, an idealized version around many of these energies that you have worshiped as gods.

The predominant energy on this planet siphons your belief systems according to its own will. It directs incredible flows of energy outward, and this energy is alive. You have been told that all of your thoughts make a world: *they are real—they go some-place.* There are five and a half billion people thinking right now. That much energy is alive on Earth. What is the predominant feeling within that energy, and what can this energy be convinced or coerced to exhibit?

We are not here to say who is right and who is wrong and who is who within the hierarchy. We simply want to bust your illusions, to pop your balloons about what you have been led to believe. We do not want to say that it is wrong; we simply want to suggest to you that you *think bigger.*

Feel the noticeable loss that is going to occur within this predominant energy when more and more of you don't vibrate according to its plan. Think what you can do when you overcome the frequency modulation or the insistence of your logical mind and when, with impeccability, you stand clean as a Keeper of Frequency. Remember that identity as a frequency is the sum total of your physical, mental, emotional, and spiritual bodies broadcast as electromagnetic pulsations. Every time you begin to own what someone has been siphoning off and to cultivate it according to your own will, you change the vibration on the planet.

As systems busters, this is one of the things that you are profoundly proficient in. We do not want to discredit or discount what you have used up until now as tools, we simply want you to outgrow your old tools. Some of your reverence and loyalty has been to belief systems that will no longer serve you, just as there will come a time when each of you will move beyond the steps that we are leading you through at this time. Another energy will be able to say, "Well, when the Pleiadians were showing you this, it was very good. They led you here and there. Let us take you further." There is no stopping the evolution, for there is nothing that has been given to the planet that represents the ultimate in truth.

As you summon the story of your reptilian past, you will find that many of the influential characters in the patriarchal system of history have indeed been part of the reptile family. Just as all humans are not bad, it is the same with the reptilians. They are no less a part of Prime Creator than you are, and their visage and physiology is not one of lesser means. Master geneticists are capable of occupying many different forms. It is quite understood that part of the difficulty of working with an isolated species is the shock that can occur with the complete revelation of truth.

There have been many other creator gods, only some of which have had human form. Presently, your greatest state of unrest or discomfort comes from beings of a reptilian type of existence because they seem the most foreign to you.

It has been our intention to expand your ideas of who your gods are because those gods will be returning to Earth. That is why the planet is going through such great turmoil. As you learn to hold the frequencies coming from the creative cosmic rays, you will be prepared to meet these gods. As we have said, some of them are already here. They walk your streets and participate in your academies, your government, and your workplaces. They are here to observe, and they are here to direct energy. Some come for great assistance, and some are here to learn and evolve. Some do not have the highest of intentions.

You must understand how to discern the extraterrestrial energies. This is a free-will universe, so all forms of life are allowed here. If an energy attempts to frighten you, manipulate you, or control you, it is not an energy that would be in your highest interest to work with. You have a choice of who you work with. Just because someone has evolved many fantastic and seemingly magic abilities does not necessarily mean that that entity is evolved spiritually. Learn to discern.

You are living in a most important time when energy is coming alive. All you are feeling is the result of you coming alive and awakening to your hidden potentials. The wind is whipping around, showing you there are great stirrings in the air. The gods are here. *You* are these gods.

As you awaken to your history, you will begin to open your ancient eyes. These are the eyes of Horus, which see not through the eyes of a human being but from the point of view of a god. They see the connectedness and purpose of all things, for the ancient eyes are able to see into many realities and to connect the whole picture, the whole history. When you open the ancient eyes within yourselves, you will not only be able to connect with your own whole personal history, you will be able to connect with the planetary history, the galactic history, and the universal history. Then, indeed, you will find out who your gods are.

FOUR

Memories in the Free-Will Zone

Once upon a time, there were beings who wanted to create something. In order to do this, they needed to go in and very subtly change a part of creation. These beings worked for, were associated with, and carefully guarded an aspect of consciousness called light. At different times, these Guardians of Light met and worked together and crossed paths in the different realms of reality. They planned, they shared blueprints, and they designed a time when their plan would go into effect.

Certain members of this light team plotted the probabilities of Prime Creator: what Prime Creator would do, where Prime Creator would act, and how Prime Creator would be stimulated. These entities understood what could be done with light, and their plan was very carefully orchestrated. For several hundred thousand years, these beings of light were trained to carry out this plan. Part of the plan involved being ready for a cosmic jolt that they anticipated would eventually be coming from Prime Creator.

There was a great deal of dedication and preparation as the groundwork was laid and the training begun. There was much to be learned before this plan could be implemented, for it was a daring plan. It was the intention of these Guardians of Light to take light, or knowledge, into a reality where that light was not welcomed and did not fit. It was like putting your foot in a shoe that does not fit.

These beings had a plan to prepare for the time when that light *would* fit. *These beings are you, and that time is now.* The time has been carefully orchestrated, and each of you knows in the deepest portions of your being that you have come here for a purpose. You have come to begin the pivotal movement to release everything that has bound you up until now into your reality, that has held you with fine threads like steel cords and locked you into ideas about yourselves and your relationship to the cosmos.

For those of you who have come to act out your plan and to work with the consciousness of light, your time is *now.* Your action springs from this moment. All you need to do is begin to allow this energy to come into your body. You must begin to vibrate with this energy and to clear the passages of the self, the emotional energies that hold themselves locked in your physical body. As you begin to examine the self, you will find that there are many selves in which to travel on the inner highways or inner nervous system of consciousness.

You will find that your society has been very cleverly designed to keep you from knowing this most intimate and rewarding and exciting portion of yourself. As Guardians of Light, you are going to create options of reality and bring them to the mass consciousness of the planet. You will do this by first doing it for yourself, creating an inner peace and inner love by accepting who you are and all that you have done in life and all that has been done to you in life. You will accept and integrate these things because you will know they have been exactly the situations necessary to bring you into this final stage of anchoring light.

This story is an ancient one, and it is stored within your body. Part of what we are requesting of you and reminding you is to open this historical treasure house and become an inner archaeologist. Be willing to travel the roads of memory of this lifetime and many other lifetimes so that you can begin to have a picture of the purpose of consciousness.

When you begin to picture the purpose of your own consciousness, and you discover the clever ways you have traveled, the many guises you have used, and the many actions you have participated in, you will learn to accept the totality of your being. When you are able to accept behavior that was not uplifting behavior, and accept your own identity of sexuality, and accept how you valued or did not value life in many lifetimes, it will open a chakra center in your body that is located around the thymus gland, between the fourth and fifth chakras. It is through here that eventually the nervous system will open and information will flow and through here that you will begin to regenerate the body and move into unconditional love.

As you accept and explore what you have participated in, you will have a greater understanding of what is going on now on the planet. You will then allow others to dance to whatever tune they are best learning from at this time. There are some pretty chaotic tunes being played upon this planet, and there is a purpose to all of them. The purpose is to strengthen the self so that the self can become completely informed about reality. The self can then decide with clarity the soul's path, or your personal path, through reality.

The original plan was for Earth to be an exchange center of information for all the different galactic systems. The Original Planners have not given up this plan. They were members of the Family of Light, and some of you have been very intimate with these Original Planners. Feel that for a moment.

We want to awaken your memories. We want you to begin to understand the magnitude of what is occurring to your species on this planet so that you can operate with comfort, knowledge, and knowing. The Original Planners are quite capable of plotting different courses and different realities.

As we have mentioned, in a free-will universe, all is allowed by Prime Creator. Therefore, since time does not exist as you know it outside of your local sector, things are left to work themselves out. So, to you humans, it seems as if it has been a long time since any kind of cosmic planetary excitement has taken place on Earth. In the larger scheme of evolution, it has not been so long, but because you are locked in the time frame of Earth, it *feels* as if it has been a long time.

Light gives information, and darkness withholds information. So, in the times that are coming, it will be easy for you to discern who's who and what's what as you travel outside the third-dimensional realm. All you need to do is discern whether something is light and you are being given information or whether it is darkness and you are being disinformed, misinformed, or information is being completely withheld from you.

Darkness and light have come from the same creator, Prime Creator, who has created a host of creator gods to go out and do its bidding. It has given all these creator gods freedom to form worlds: to discover how to create life, how to become responsible stewards of life, and how to become parents for the planets in the galactic systems that they have created. Learning to become a good parent has been a constant ongoing process.

The creator gods have taken themselves and made themselves and fed their worlds from themselves. In Egypt, there is a story about a creator god who masturbated and created the world. The god took himself and made small identities out of himself so that he could be in what he made and not outside of it.

You are all needed to access the portion of memory that is part of the creator gods. Who are these gods? Who are the gods that fought with these gods? Who are some of the gods who came here and controlled you? Part of your task is to access your memory.

When these beings return to Earth, there will be many of you who will turn to them and say, "Yes, these are wonderful gods. I feel wonderful about them. They are so magnificent. Look what they can do." Some of these gods will seem to fix and save your world. This is where it will be easy to miss the bigger picture. It will *look* as if they are coming to fix and save your world when, in actuality, what they are doing is simply creating another form of authority and control. What we are saying is that people will put a belief system and a paradigm on these entities. There will be a large marketing program to sell the presence of these entities to you. This program is already going on. You are not like the masses on Earth, for you are members of the Family of Light, and you *know* things that others do not. You may know that these beings are not of light, and you may know it to the core of your being. You may become sickened in a society that does not know this. Many people will turn to worshiping these beings because it will seem as if miracles are occurring and the grandest event in the history of the world is taking place. It may seem that humanity is being given a whole new opportunity, a whole new golden era. Then there will be a very big surprise, and people will find that the tyrannies are larger than ever before.

The purpose, of course, is for each individual to become sovereign *and* for the planet to unite. Not everyone is going to make the shift. Everyone is not in the vibration that wants to work in harmony at this time. There are those on Earth who will feel as if they are in states of ecstasy when they find what they think is a new authority, a higher authority, a new paradigm, animal gods, or whatever. So the Family of Light, as it has infiltrated and penetrated this planet, is going to create its own planetary sphere, its own Earth.

You are all learning about authority. Who is the boss for the beings who are here now? Who is *their* God? Who is their authority? That authority is coming back to Earth. There is a lesson in this for Earth. These beings, who are neither spiritually informed nor lean in spiritual ways, deny the existence of a spiritual force. They have developed scientific principles and technologies that scatter the laws of spirituality.

You may think that because you understand or believe in the spiritual realms that every person, as they evolve, will naturally embrace that information. It is not so. It is possible to become a brilliant master of manipulating matter and reality without understanding spiritual connections. It is very important that you learn this.

There will be those who will come from the stars to this planet who will have abilities that will be incredible to the mass consciousness of the people upon Earth. But these beings will not feel, for they will not be connected to any spiritual seeking. The choice to seek, to awaken the spiritual self, is, of course, free to each person upon this planet and to each person in this whole universe. Not everyone is going to realize it.

Just as you have cultivated very powerful individuals upon this planet who are not in touch with their feeling centers—who have no connection to emotional and spiritual consciousness— there are those who exist in space who are extremely powerful space kings or space entities who have nothing to do with spirituality. They are powerful forces. If you met these forces, you would feel like David meeting Goliath. That is why it is important for all of you to learn how to alter your reality so that you can dance between the vibrations of frequency, or flip into the station of the world that you want to experience.

Wanting to have something to worship is the frequency control on Earth. What the planet is headed for is someone or something new to worship. That is the potential holographic insert—*a new god to worship.* The creator gods, the reptiles, know that their plan has run short, so to speak, and there is an intention of creating a new plan, a new diversion, a new disempowerment. Therefore, beyond anything else, *listen to yourselves.* Listen to the internal message that comes through to you and begin to dance with it and make friends with it. You, yourselves, are meant to discover reality from *inside* and to direct your life in this way. This is really the gift that is given in the free-will zone.

Part of the dichotomy or balancing in a free-will zone is the allowance of *all things,* even tyrannies. In this free-will zone, everyone is endowed with the potential to create their own reality. It is a free-will choice to create having someone else create reality for you. Most people on Earth allow others to create and dictate their reality to them. Through frequency control, you have been steered to look *outside of yourself* for answers. When new gods appear, you are ready to worship them. It goes on and on. Those who control frequency in this way are lost in the same thing, and you are their mirror.

As you begin to live according to your own guidance and your own daring, everything changes completely. This is occurring in many places. Just as thought travels on Earth, there are highways on which thought can be directed throughout the cosmos. The gridworks and creative cosmic rays are part of an intergalactic system that directs what you believe into other places of existence. So even today you are a living inspiration to others as a frequency that is fed into other systems.

In the same way that we pull energy from other systems into your system, you send energy to other systems and affect them—and you don't know it. We want you to realize your impact and the power you have to affect systems. You don't even know how powerful you are, and that is why you could be dangerous. You have taken on an incredible amount of this mutating energy. What are you going to do with it? How are you going to direct it? Do you love yourself?

The Original Planners are after much more than this particular zone here: they are after a shift in the universal DNA. They want the entire universe to orchestrate a new symphony in consciousness. They are not only after the reestablishment of frequency availability on Earth. Their game is much bigger: they are after a restructuring of the vibratory rate of this entire universe. They are creating this by going into key zones to infiltrate and bring about a simultaneous implosion. There will be a universal awakening within these various centers so that the entire universe will change its frequency in its own time.

The Original Planners have solicited the interest of Prime Creator. Prime Creator learns from all things that exist because it *is* all things. Just as you are learning to honor your lessons, the things that you manifest for yourself, Prime Creator honors all creations. Prime Creator lets its creations *be* and learns about its own potential by watching what it has birthed, just as a wise parent learns from its children. Prime Creator needs you to go out and bring the newest inventions unto it so that it can experience and evolve.

Prime Creator has turned its energy toward this free-will zone because, from a vast point in your future, it has been shown where this experiment will go if left unchecked and unattended. Energy could simply run rampant and own other energy. There is a vast probability that reaches out for hundreds and thousands of years of a dictatorship in this universal system. From a place far into the future, this experiment is being reworked: its essential energy is being transmuted and transformed. You are a part of that transformation by going into the bowels of the system in various disguises and becoming awakened.

The human portion of you has delineated who is a good guy and who is a bad guy and who is who in the space hierarchy. There have been tremendous amounts of literature on this subject, and you have bought it all. Smash all of those ideas. Smash every one of them, *including* who you think we are.

Over the next number of years, those who come from the skies may not be members of the Family of Light. They will be the mirror of those upon the planet. We have said to you that your lesson is authority—to become your own authority and to stop giving over your decision-making process to governmental people or parents or teachers or gods. *It is time for the people of Earth to become sovereign.*

Humans are going to need to be tricked before they can become aware. Many of you may find that you will be very frustrated. You will see things that others will not see; you will see a mass mania occurring upon this planet, and you will not be able to live with it. You will see masses of people walk toward a false god that is foolishness.

You are beginning to feel what may be coming. It is an awesome task to carry light: once you put it in your body, there is no stopping it. There is no saying, "I quit the light team. I won't be recognized as a member of the Family of Light." Some of you may want to do this sometimes, but once light is there, that is it.

We want you to realize that those space beings on and

around this planet who you feel are "bad guys"—and with whom your government forces have made deals—are dealing with the same issues that you are. They are beings who are reflecting your beliefs and drama back at you. They have been accused of heinous behavior, of performing mutations and abductions upon the human species, which has sent out a cry among many of the organizational members of UFO study.

Yet, these beings act as a mirror to show you your own world: what you acquiesce to and what you acquiesce to let your leaders do all over the world. How is your acquiescence to the government and media, and the way you are used, different from a cow who is mutilated by an extraterrestrial? These extraterrestrials who come here do nothing different than your own species does. The masses allow the leaders to do as they wish in their name because the masses do not rise up and say, "Hey, I do not approve of this!" There is a complacency upon Earth. The consciousness on this planet is, "You do it for me. I don't want to be responsible. You become my government official. You become my teacher. You become my boss. *Someone tell me what to do.*"

These extraterrestrials mirror this to you. Remember the movie *V* that was shown on television a few years ago? That movie gives you some idea of the cunning and conniving of certain entities who will come from space; some people will indeed worship them and think they are absolutely powerful masters. We are saying that these scenarios are going to prove true. There is a pending merging of human consciousness and the extraterrestrial presence upon this planet. It is being marketed to you at a rapid rate.

Many of you who have studied and used your own discernment will be shocked and appalled at the foolishness and ideological worship that the rest of the human race will express toward certain beings from space who pass themselves off as your creators even though they do not have bodies that look like yours. They will be able to do many things and will share many technologies. They will perhaps cure certain diseases that they helped create in the first place by teaching germ warfare to your planetary scientists.

You will become disgusted with society because you will not fit with the new gods, and you will retreat. Do you understand that the new gods may be lizards? You think that's a little funny? Hold onto your seats, because you have no idea what is coming. If we told you everything that was coming, you would have scattered a long time ago.

There are some who play on both teams because they are double agents. This is very complicated, and it is time for you to understand it. We are pushing your paradigms and stretching your identity because we are preparing you for something. If you are prepared, you will be able to stand firmly in an identity and not be crushed by what you thought was out there.

Oh, dear humans, you are in for an adventure, and only *you* can carry this adventure out. The nonphysical realms continuously support you, and members of the Family of Light are around you and with you all the time. Yet, it is up to you to master the laws that we share with you and to anchor them upon this planet.

When you begin to live all that we teach you—to trust identity, to trust synchronicity, to trust being a part of a plan—then you will find that even in the midst of great calamity and incredible odds you will be able to defy the laws of humanity.

The creator gods have their own creators toward whom they are evolving. The lapse in consciousness between the creator gods and their creators occurred within the context of the manipulation of worlds and universes, not necessarily the manipulation of species. You, as a species, are being manipulated within a multitude of realities. It is your task to figure out how many realities you exist within. For those beings who are manipulating you, their task is to realize how many worlds they are manipulating realities in. The creator gods are jugglers of realities, but who is juggling their realities and putting them through their creation in all of these worlds in the first place?

All of this is to be *felt*. Allow your brain cells to click into being without your rational, conscious mind wanting to define things down to the most minute detail. This experience involves raising a feeling inside yourself and then, one day, at one moment, in one afternoon, having an overwhelming sense of *knowing*: having a composition a thousand pages long come alive in five seconds of divine ecstasy.

FIVE

Who Carries the Chord of Light?

You hold the history of the universe within your physical body. What is occurring upon the planet now is the literal mutation of your physical body, for you are allowing it to be evolved to a point where it will be a computer that can house this information.

This is going to occur due to biogenetic engineering that really has nothing to do with you. You can facilitate the process, of course, by intending cooperation with it. As a species, you are being biogenetically altered by the beings who created you and who redesign your DNA at periodic junctures in your history.

This time period was designed by the original creator gods or project designers for them to come back and take over this place and return it to its original plan. Millions have been called to participate in this project. Millions have said, "Yes, we are renegades. Let us go and take back this project and see if we can set it right. We will rebuild the ruins and put it together."

So the plans have been drawn and the designs made and the genetics studied to find who carries the recessive genes and the chord of light inside them. You have selected with great clarity the parentage that genealogically provides you with the fullest accessibility to combinations of light-encoded filaments that can potentially evolve.

Before you came into the body, all of you committed to designing events that would fire your codings, or blueprints—

that would activate your memories. Then you came into the body and you forgot. All of you have had your blueprints and codings fired to some extent because you understand that there is a divine purpose or Divine Plan that you are a part of. The firing of the codings and the realization of your identity are going to become phenomenally intense. The reason for this is the evolving DNA. When you have twelve helixes of DNA in place, those helixes will begin to plug into the twelve-chakra system.

The twelve chakras are vortex centers loaded with information that you must be able to translate. You are evolving yourself even when you are not on the planet and you are perhaps more involved with other identities of yourself. Therefore, to evolve, you pick particularly challenging situations in which you have to rise beyond what has been established as a ceiling or boundary of what is possible. You have to become super beings in whatever reality you enter because, as members of the Family of Light, the branch of renegades, this is your forté. You purposely came to this planet to give yourself such a challenge so that you could be defiant—not in a way that would give you problems or create disharmony, but in a way that would create *harmonic defiance*. Through your harmony, you are defiant toward the old vibrational frequency.

Part of the friction you feel with others is that you are on this path of evolution and bursting forth. Others don't like this because they are not coded at this time to respond the way you are. Some people are not coded at all for this. Some knew the plan of change and came here at this time to be observers. Some timid beings came here knowing that if they had the courage to step onto this planet—while realizing what the blueprint of the planet was—that somehow this would be an accreditation of their own conscious journey and would catapult them into higher consciousness even if their only participation in the transition was simply to be here.

Just to be in the vicinity of this kind of activity is empowering. So give due credit to all who are on the planet at this time who have decided to be participants in this great frequency change. All of these participants are necessary, because the more frequencies that are on the planet, the more energy that can build to alter the old frequency. Those who have opened themselves to light are literally having their bodies rearranged. Sometimes you may wake up at night and literally feel the rearrangement. This rearrangement of the body is the restructuring of the DNA.

Your DNA is a filament; a scientist would describe it as a connective filament. Scientists, doing the best they can up to this point, have found certain codings within certain portions of the DNA. They have also found superfluous portions of the DNA. In other words, there are portions that they cannot translate or figure out, so they think these portions of the DNA are just there for the ride, and they call them "junk DNA." They are off track.

We have talked about how all of you were built by the creator gods. You were built like houses that were going to be expanded or added on to in the future. You are now at that juncture when those who designed you are adding on to who you are. What the scientists call "junk DNA" has been dormant in your body for a long time, and it is now becoming activated. In our teachings, we always emphasize the importance of oxygenation, because oxygen feeds the coding and awakens the junk DNA in your body (which certainly isn't junk at all).

What scientists are calling "junk" houses the perceptions deep inside of your body that will allow you to become an entire perceiver, a fourth-dimensional being. This awakening DNA will allow you to change your eyesight, change your hearing, increase your life span, and so on. This dormant part of the DNA that has baffled the scientists is now coming to life.

You are mutating so quickly now that certain scientists call the process a disease. Some are very concerned about it. They have persuaded the government to invest billions of dollars to research DNA. What is occurring in your body is certainly not a disease: you are being naturally mutated and rearranged. This mutation occurs most often while you are sleeping, so you may be waking up in the mornings noticing that something feels a little different in your body. You can expect that the changes will begin to show themselves and that you will develop new abilities. You will automatically *know* many things.

The original designers of the human body were benevolent beings. These original creator gods were very generous in endowing you biogenetically with a tremendous vitality of spirit and a tremendous zest of capability. Much of this information is stored within your body in the light-encoded filaments that are scattered and are coming back into alignment. Your bones and skeletal form correspond with that information. When your skeletal form is in alignment, the energy from sacred power sites is released, the cosmic rays are pulled into your body, and the light-encoded filaments inside your cells begin to reorder themselves, you will find that you are in the change. The change will be mirrored to you everywhere you look.

The present evolutionary system designed by the creator gods to step you up a number of dimensions or frequencies is based upon the evolution of the twelve helixes that correspond to the twelve chakra centers—seven within your body and five outside your body. This is simply the way the system plugs in. With respect to the evolution of the helixes within the human body, a common denominator frequency must be attained that even those in the lowest possible stations can reach.

There are also those humans who could go beyond the twelve helixes. In general, however, the state of consciousness of humanity cannot achieve that kind of acceleration. It is enough of a leap for people to go from a double-helix system to a twelve-helix system.

Some people will be functioning with the twelve helixes within a short period of time, while others around the planet will not receive this shift until later in the decade. This is simply because each individual is coded to be given the frequency when they are capable of integrating it. Many are already having a difficult time integrating the changes at this early stage of the plan. A large majority of the humans on Earth have convinced themselves that there is only one reality and there can be no other. This could be the downfall of the human race.

As the helixes come into full force in a person, there is an awakening of the person's inner knowledge, knowledge that goes beyond what the person has been taught. This inner knowledge is knowledge of self, knowledge that says there is much more than this physical world. *Believe it. Know it. Understand it.*

The physical world is a clue to the spiritual world. The world of spirit and self-evolution is on the verge of an information explosion: cheap energy, free energy—everything will be given to you. All of this is related to the evolving light-encoded filaments, which are millions and billions of tiny little fibers.

As we related the story to you, the raiding creator gods who came in and took over needed to have you operate in a certain way in order to control you. They needed to unplug your intelligence, and so they did, by scattering and disconnecting the light-encoded filaments that form the helixes in your DNA. These filaments are now beginning to reconnect into helixes. The helixes will evolve in sets of three until there are twelve strands, or helixes. When these twelve helixes or strands of many light-encoded filaments begin to vibrate within the body, each of the strands will correspond to a chakra center.

There are multitudes of chakra centers, and there are multitudes of potential helixes that can form. Right now, the common denominator with respect to the number of helixes and chakras that the consciousness of humanity can handle without destroying itself is twelve. So we are dealing right now with an evolvement of twelve helixes to plug into the twelve chakras— as mentioned before, seven chakras in the body and five chakras outside the body. The seven chakras in the body are not too difficult to work with because, if you allow yourself to feel, you can physically touch and locate all of them. The first three are the chakras of survival, sexuality, and perceptual feeling. The fourth chakra is the heart—center of compassion and connectedness to all things. The fifth is the throat chakra, which relates to speaking. The sixth is the third eye, the vision. The seventh is the crown chakra, which opens to the knowing that one's identity goes beyond the physical form. When you get to the five outside of the body, you must begin to find new ways to figure out what is going on with something that you don't even know for sure is real.

The eighth chakra is within your realm of activity. It hovers twelve inches or more above your head. Most people keep the eighth chakra center close to their physical body. The ninth chakra is close as well, within a few feet of the body. Once nine helixes are formed, this chakra will move out into the atmosphere of Earth to become more of an Earth chakra, connecting into the gridwork. It is a link.

The tenth, eleventh, and twelfth chakras are much further out. The tenth chakra, once it is in line and plugged in, will be in your solar system. The eleventh chakra will move out into your galactic system, and the twelfth will be located and anchored some place in this universe.

You will receive information from these personal centers, for they are collective centers as well, just as your other personal chakra centers are collective centers. As you learn to translate the chakra experiences, you will discover that life is not the same anymore.

Not all people on the planet are going through these changes right now, because you are not all coded to respond at this particular time. Each of you came in with a certain order—a map of when and where and how you best operate. Many of you are learning how to follow this plan of the self that will lead you to discover your exalted self. Once you learn how to do this, life will become quite effortless because you will become a vehicle for light and you will be moved just by your intention to commit.

Different humans will be exposed to these changes at different times because it would not do to have them occur all at once. This would create chaos, where a certain order is needed. As an individual goes through the changes and translates the experience, they can turn to someone to assist them who has already gone through the changes. For those of you who are the beginning people, the process can be very difficult. You are the way showers. Once you are able to go through the changes, you can make the path and show others. There are road maps that indicate certain events that can occur if you wish to plug into those gridworks of time. The greater commitment you have in every moment to your own evolution, the sooner the changes will occur for the last person.

There was a time when the human species occupied higher dimensional frequencies and you had the ability to move through realities and manipulate matter. Many of these abilities were purposely scattered by those beings who are in charge of your reality. You must understand that every reality has its guardians and that there are different stewardships and guardians at different times.

We are using the term *guardian* in a neutral fashion. You use the term *guardian* for someone who is protective. We will say that a guardian is in charge of reality and that perhaps they guard it from others; they don't let others come in and change their reality. Guardians, as we are referring to them, are not necessarily benevolent, uplifting entities. The entities who are guarding your reality could be keeping out those entities who would set you free.

You have forgotten so much because you were retooled, and many of your inherent abilities were scattered and unplugged so that they would not work. Control came down over minds in your society. There are veils of protection that were put around Earth, because if you were to attempt to plug into some of this information, you would not have the tools or the background or the ability to make sense of these realities.

Now the whole planet is immersed in expanding realities. In order to go into these other realities, you will first need to explore very deeply your own reality. There is no time to have twenty years of psychoanalysis. You have to develop skills and abilities within a few hours that will allow you to travel a few decades in your own emotional evolution. You are going to have to travel the emotional highway, because the human body expresses itself through the emotions. That is the uniqueness and gift of your species.

First you will need to open the emotional highways to areas that you have hidden from yourself in this particular lifetime. Memories may flood in as this data is lined up inside you—memories about events that were difficult for you at the time or perhaps that you did not have a context for. Some of you may uncover the events of extraterrestrial contact that all of you had when you were children. Some of you may uncover expressions of sexuality that you did not understand at the time you were involved in them, whether you were a passive or an active participant. Such things have been buried by the human emotional body because it is very sensitive to judgment, and the mental body passes tremendous judgment. The emotional body, linked to the spiritual body, hides from this.

You all think you know who you are. You have stories of who you are based upon what you remember of growing up in this lifetime. What we want to communicate to you is that you have a number of parallel, legitimate existences that have different memories than you have. You stopped these memories or didn't focus on the related events because your emotional body could not compute them.

Much of what you will tap into is tied to your sexuality because it is a part of yourself that you have not understood and that you must go into in order to understand its purpose. What is sexuality all about? Who made these rules about the appropriate and inappropriate expression of it? Also coming up for you will be the realization of the contacts and energy that were continuously around many of you when you were younger to teach you; you blocked out these events because you were not given the support to believe they truly occurred.

As you begin this multidimensional exploration, the memories that you have hidden from yourself will come forward. You will be astounded that you could have completely forgotten whole events and large chunks of your life, especially events that occurred when you were under twelve years old. You will be amazed when you explore the ability of the nervous system to shut down the flow of data that the mind cannot compute. And yet, the records are there, so you will replay them. You now will have the ability to compute many of these things because you are will learn to be neutral and not to judge what you have participated in.

As you explore your current body, identity, and lifetime, do it quickly. You do not have years to study them. As the information in your DNA is retooled and replugged in, you will be able to feel how the events from this life connect and blossom and have a thread of purpose with many different places that you have lived and many different identities that you have occupied.

Ideally, you will move out of judgment, and because of that you will be able to pick up the story of what really happened here, which you will experience firsthand through cellular memory. The only way you can step into this higher frequency and determine the future of your lives on this planet is to *not judge your participation within this process.* This is very complex and very important: *feel* what we just said. This process involves smashing the existing paradigm and becoming a heretic of reality. You will begin to understand that a legitimate, real existence has simply been hidden from you. *It is imperative that you begin to remember who you are.*

You are not alone. You could not do this alone. Even when we say to you that you are the standard bearer of your soul, there are other aspects of yourself that have figured the story out and are coming back into your time period to create this vortex of energy that is going to affect all realities. We cannot emphasize enough the importance of these times and the excitement and joy of what they hold—*as long as you are willing to change.*

If you are not willing to change and not willing to give things up, you will have to go through experiences that will be less than joyful. All of you will have certain things you may not want to give up. That may be the difficulty, for each of you has your area of clutching and clinging. And yet, each of you came to do something here so that you could get on with your travels and with what your soul is craving to experience. It is as if you have unfinished business here. The veil for many of you was pulled down very tightly so that you would not fly away and say, "What am I doing here again? I'm out of here!"

Those of you who understand the higher realms have many times felt very alone here upon the planet. There are millions like you here at this time, forming a tremendous support group. You are beginning to meet and find one another, and you are beginning to thread your consciousness—one fine silk strand with other strands of consciousness. You will see a most beautiful creation come together without great effort because it is part of a plan and you are moved to do certain things.

The whole planet has been controlled in such a way that you have been taught and trained from the time you first arrived here that you are not in control of your own reality. You have been taught that everything is circumstantial and that everything depends on something you have no say in. This is *wrong!* You are the one who controls your DNA.

You have complete control over everything. Until you discover that and believe it, you are subjected to whatever anyone else wishes to do to you in this free-will zone. And, in your innocence, you have been exposed to things that have allowed your DNA, your intelligence, and many other things to be controlled.

SIX

Unlocking the History

DNA carries the coding, for this genetic material and its helixes are made up of light-encoded filaments—tiny gossamer threads that carry information the way fiber optics systems do. The pillar of light that you use to activate yourself and to bring information into your body is also composed of light-encoded filaments. These light-encoded filaments carry a vast amount of data and information, and your body is filled with them. When bundled together and placed in a certain alignment, the light-encoded filaments work together and release information that makes sense of the history they carry.

The light-encoded filaments inside your body are similar to a grand library—a library that is so gigantic it carries the history of your universe. During the course of the Earth's history, there have been many different species who have lived here. You have convinced yourself that humanity is native to this planet. *Human beings were put here.* People are in for a shock because they are going to discover very shortly the skeletal forms of very different creatures. Some of these have already been discovered, particularly in South America, though they have been either written up in your tabloid newspapers and passed off as a hoax or fearfully kept in secret. When the consciousness of humanity is raised to the frequency of receptivity, and the nervous system of the mass psyche is balanced to the point that you can have a paradigm shift, Earth itself will reveal its secrets through a variety of means such as weather patterns, Earth changes, psychic discoveries, and so on. You will unearth a whole new history. The task you have before you is to consciously command, intend, and will the evolvement of your DNA. Commanding and willing and asking for this is not easy, for you must move through many identities. From the historical perspective of your multidimensional existence or essence or soul, you have been all kinds of characters, and some of these experiences have been painful. They have been challenging and difficult.

It is time for you to move through the challenges and unlock the history that is inside of your body by allowing the light-encoded filaments to rebundle, forming new helixes, and by allowing yourself to be receptive to what this new information in the DNA is going to plug in to you. It will not always make sense to your logical mind. You will learn that your logical mind has a place, a function, and a purpose, but that it is not your identity. The logical mind is overused by many people. It is overtaxed and abused, and when you overuse and abuse the logical mind, you create stress upon your body. You do not always need to understand logically what you are experiencing. Watch yourself, maintain humor at all times, and maintain the idea that you are evolving.

You will be going through many things because you are climbing a ladder of identity made up of your chakra system. The chakras are energy information centers that are keyed into lifetimes in which you activated or expressed yourself in one area or another. It is imperative for you to discover your identity in these next few years.

The light-encoded filaments are a tool of light, a part of light, and an expression of light. These light-encoded filaments exist as millions of fine, threadlike fibers inside your cells, while counterpart light-encoded filaments exist outside of your body. The light-encoded filaments carry the Language of Light geometry, which carries the stories of who you are. These light-encoded filaments were not previously able to come onto the planet because there was a pollution created by the dark team that kept them out.

The light-encoded filaments are like rays of light that hold a geometric form of language. They come to you from a cosmic database and hold information. Many of you are at the point where you don't need to have a healing done on your body. You need to have a spontaneous education, or implant, put into your body to teach you. This is what will be coming during the next number of years.

Some of the people on this planet, particularly those working with crystals, will learn to fill and activate other bodies with these filaments. Individuals seeking this experience will have the filaments activated in their bodies to give them instant information and instant knowing. This is what education is evolving into. There will be beings who will assist you with all of this. You are going to have to be able to recognize these beings and to recognize other realities as they exist around you.

When the information in the light-encoded filaments was scattered, there was no burning of the libraries—it was simply that all of the books were torn off the shelves and left in the center of the room. Imagine if you walked into a room the size of a gigantic stadium and all of the books or information it had been filled with was pulled off the shelves and left in the middle of the floor. How could you find anything except by chance? Since humans don't believe in the order of chance, they have never followed the order that is within them.

The information in the filaments was left inside of you, yet there was no *logical* way to make sense of it. So, in the present time, how do you find the information? The information is going to reveal itself to you. That is the process. You don't have to go looking for it because this revelation is your heritage and who you are. As the DNA begins to form new strands, these new strands will travel along a nervous system in the body that is being developed at this time, and memories will come flooding into your consciousness. You must work to develop this nervous system, to pull light into your body, to oxygenate your system, to learn how to move through energy accelerations, and to call more ideas and experiences into your body. As this process begins to grow and nurture itself in your body, simply observe it, for you will want to know how to access it. Getting stuck in your dramas is like reading one of your books over and over again and not letting all of the information in other books come together. There is more: *there is a whole story.*

This whole story has to do with your entire soul. As members of the Family of Light, you are agreeing to hold in your physical bodies a conscious awareness of all of your existences. You are agreeing to accept what you have done and the parts you have played in all these existences and then to raid differ-ent realities and change them according to the dictates of your agreement as a representative of the Family of Light. You have free will within this agreement, of course.

The triple helix brings you into the feeling center. The feeling center is emotion, and emotion is your road or bridge or *ticket to the spiritual self.* When people deny the emotional self, they can't get in to the spiritual realms. The Christed one said, "Know thyself." *Know thyselves.* It's the same thing. That message was given on the planet a long time ago, but it was distorted so that people could not understand how grand indeed they were and that all they had to do was rearrange themselves.

The work is always internal. When you want to know how to go about bringing a change upon the planet, we always tell you to *work with yourself.* Develop yourself. Move beyond the boundaries of self. Learn to become multidimensional, to exist in the astral world, and to travel beyond the physical body. Stop defining the body as ending "here," which is what society encourages you to do so that you can be controlled. In a free-will zone, control is part of the game because someone wants to be in charge. You are members of the Family of Light. To what hierarchy and to what gods do you answer?

DNA is a living history of truth and life. When one is able to merge with this history, one is able to go into realities without videos, tapes, or books. One is able to *experience.* Many native cultures were trained to find the remnants of the Living Library left upon this planet. That explains their reverence for Earth and animals and their understanding of the cooperation that runs through everything. These native cultures were purposely put upon the planet so that there would be a training ground and a place of potential memory activation when the time was right.

DNA holds the code. It holds the blueprint of identity, the plan for existence, the history of the universe, and the history of life in this particular locale. And, it is stored within the cells of humans. The original DNA of the stewards of this planet, the human occupants, had a genetic blueprint system that was based on the number twelve. The twelve strands of genetic material are therefore connected to many other representatives or informational sources that also number twelve. Remember, reality mirrors reality. The twelve strands of information hooked the human occupant up with corresponding information centers in and out of the body.

Earth is now entering a conjunction or lineup with purpose through which the Original Planners are returning to reactivate the twelve-helix system in the occupying species—the human to date—and put Earth back on its track. When the biological library was conceived of eons and eons ago, it was decided that the stewards of the planet would hold the key to unlocking the data that was stored in this Living Library.

How does this tie in with the twelve information centers? When human chakra systems are connected, open, and activated, information starts to seek its own expression and become available. There are certain things that will code or trigger this information, bringing it to the forefront of existence to get it to begin to express itself. When you are hooked into the information centers, seven in your body and five outside your body, you are ready to receive energy through another set of twelve information centers. When you activate your own twelve chakras, you hook into energy stored in parallel sets of twelve centers that will further activate your process. This will eventually bring the brain into its complete, full, computerlike function.

The twelve parallel realities hold ways to unlock information that has been secreted away. There are many steps to unlocking this information. You could compare this to governmental deep security, which uses different levels of fingerprints and imprints to access the final bit of information. There are many different ways things must be connected if something very secret is stored away.

The activation of the twelve strands of DNA coincides with the activation, spinning, movement, and opening of the twelve centers of information—the twelve chakras or etheric energy discs. This is the beginning of the connection of the spinning of the twelve. When this alignment of energy takes place, it brings and pulls energy into the twelve heavenly bodies in your solar system. These bodies then begin to feed energy back to Earth. They activate themselves by releasing what they hold so that Earth can biogenetically come alive. There are more and more of these groups of twelve—the twelve universes spinning, for example. Through the spinning of the twelve centers, there will be a chaos of new consciousness, because when these twelve energy centers—particularly the outer five—begin to hook themselves back up with the planet, there will be an incredible flood of new energy.

The formation of the twelve helixes will not mean that you will become completely informed as a species. It means that in order to catapult the species of humans forward into a higher consciousness, there is a maximum and minimum mutation that needs to take place to create a new standard of operation. This mutation will bring in a new frequency level that each person will become affected by in their own way. The process could be compared to a new sun being born in your atmosphere. These twelve helixes certainly do not comprise all of the information inside the light-encoded filaments. However, the forming of the twelve helixes will be plenty to give you, as a species, a much bigger picture of who you are.

As members of the Family of Light, you *know* who you are. It is the humans who don't know who they are. Since you are in disguise as humans, however, sometimes you trick yourselves into thinking that you don't know who you are either. You know from the eternal portion of your being that you are a member of the Family of Light.

We call Earth the Living Library because you all have an image of what a library is: it is a place where information is stored and available. We use this analogy because we intend to evoke the image that everywhere you go you are in a library. You just haven't figured out yet how to translate the information or recognize where it is in the library.

This is the image that we would like everyone to begin to have. It will create a greater loving for Earth, and a greater realization that there is something for everyone to relate to in this place. No one need ever be alone when they find out that there is intelligent life willing to communicate with human beings. Once there is formulation of the twelve helixes, which hook one up to the twelve information centers, the library will be activated.

Humans were designed to be the key to access this information in the Living Library. There are many stories that we can go into about this. Millions of years ago, all life coexisted on this planet, particularly during the dinosaur period, when these large beasts operated as guardians of the planet and certain energies were building to store data here. For many millions of years this occurred.

Right now *twelve* is the system that connects, and if you look around, you will see it everywhere. It was a symbolic insertion for a reason: so that you would someday figure out that it connects you to something somewhere else. It is not your natural rhythm but is a group agreement to use the energy of twelve in many different systems of reality. It is a coded formula. Many things that make no sense to the logical mind make a tremendous amount of sense to the light-encoded filaments and to the body as it is becoming more sensitive.

There are those who would say that this is a very inefficient system and that it is not a natural flow. But this system of twelve is the flow that this planet was adjusted to. In actuality, if you look, you are a system of thirteen. How many times a year does the moon come full? Thirteen. The system of thirteen will come. You will open to it soon because you will move past time. The energy of thirteen moves beyond logic and beyond the forced system.

Now, as we have indicated, the Family of Light has come onto the planet to receive energy from the Original Planners. This energy will create a genetic alteration and reactivate and rebundle the light-encoded filaments. The filaments will make up the twelve-helix system that can move the body into activation. This will make human beings very valuable because they will then be ready to be used to access the data that is stored in Earth.

What is this data that is so important? It is disguised in insects and flowers and pigs and donkey tails and rabbit ears and all kinds of things, and it is for you to discover. We want to emphasize that when the data was stored in the twelve libraries, it was stored in many different layers. When you came into the libraries, there were different codes of clearance. In other words, there were many different ways of entering the libraries. You could not just walk in and say, "I have free clearance to receive all of this information." Just as there is now security clearance within your government, so the libraries holding this information had security systems.

There was reason to build the libraries in the first place, for the pulsation of tyranny was beating at the time. There was concern on the part of certain energies, the Keepers of Time, that information might get into the wrong hands. So, very playfully, libraries were designed in many different modes. The other libraries, or worlds, are not at all like your world. The task for the Keepers of Time was to engineer a project through which consciousness could evolve, have information, and be utilized to access information.

Originally, the role of the human occupant as the way shower to the library was one of great honor. Without the human occupant, one could not access the library, and the more tuned in the human occupant was, the more one could access the library. The human occupant had a certain pride in being loose enough and connected enough to find the data in all things.

If humans were the library cards, then some were better library cards than others. There was training that went into being the library card, and when beings came who wanted to find information on the planet, they would merge with the human occupant who was coded to respond to certain codes. If someone had a low code, they might only see a certain amount of something; each one came with the purpose of accessing specific information. Information was not withheld from someone because it was secretive, but because the information was not electromagnetically suited to their biological structure.

Data must be able to penetrate the belief system of an individual; otherwise, the individual could blow up if they are overwhelmed with energy that is not strongly tempered with love. When something is strongly tempered with love, it prevents the individual from blowing apart and keeps them focused on receiving a very enlarged concept. This is how large concepts are transduced onto this planet: they ride the love frequency.

Light frequency cannot carry large concepts because it is not connected with emotion. Love frequency is connected with emotion. When an individual is creating an expanded concept of themselves, there must be a love that gives the individual purpose. Without love, the individual does not feel there is purpose, and the individual must always feel connected with purpose to understand how vast things are.

You are going to discover someday that sex is part of the process. When you own your own sexuality, you will see the opportunities you have to express it, and you will decide whether you want to express it in those ways or not. As you become accessible, and as others utilize you to discover the library, you may have very interesting encounters as the years evolve. If you go back and study the scriptures and ancient manuscripts, you will understand that the gods came down and intermingled with the daughters of human beings.

Sexuality has been used to spark the library card. There is something very dangerous in this, however, because it has been misused. That is why it is very important to *own* your sexuality and be very certain whom you share it with. We don't want any of you to be in a position to be bought or enticed. You are advised to look and see if you experience others as being honest and having integrity or whether they are flattering you. You are becoming stewards for power.

There are traditionalists who feel we are making entirely too much information available without supervision. We say that Earth is headed for a major collision, so no holds barred. We are flooding the planet, as are many others, with opportunities to remember. So, as you begin to amass this knowledge and these abilities, there will be others attracted to you for their own reasons because of what they can access through you.

When you are sexual with someone, it is like opening an avenue to the other libraries. It has to do with many, many things. Part of what we want all of you to do is love and honor your bodies, love yourself, and make certain that if you are going to be sexual with someone that the person *really love you*. It doesn't mean you are going to marry them. But there has to be love so that you know who you are bonding with; in this way, the discoveries that you make move between the two of you. We are not so much warning you as we are informing you, because you will see things happen to others who are not careful of their power.

In other words, sexuality is not something to fool around with. It is a way to open many avenues. If one does not approach it carefully, one can attract energies even without having a partner. If one is using sexuality to activate information, one could invite the wrong energies in. So be aware of the frequency of sexuality, because it brings up the emotions, and the emotions are the key to accessing the data that is stored in the Living Library.

SEVEN

The Multidimensional Merge

You benefit by participating in the event of life. By simply being *in* physicality, you are endowed with experiences and characteristics that you cannot gather anywhere else. To be part of physicality on Earth at this particular time and during the last 200,000 to 300,000 years is a very potent event indeed, because it means that you have come into a place where darkness has been reigning. You have had to struggle to open your eyes in any capacity and to recognize joy and upliftment. If you think back over modern history, you will find that it has been a rare event indeed for people to have had uplifting lives. Therefore, you must birth upliftment for yourself, and you must convince yourself that you can do it.

The nature of existence on Earth has been a struggle between light and darkness for many eons. Some would call it a struggle between good and bad, or upliftment and evil. We will simply say that it is an event and place where certain laws and rules exist and that Earth is certainly not the only place in existence that deals with these kinds of challenges.

You are unique in that the biogenetic structure you operate within has much greater capability than you have ever dreamed of. It is so interesting to watch you perform within these struggles, because you have been convinced that you can utilize only a small percentage of your potential. In actuality, you are grand creatures designed in the image of gods. Even gifted with this incredible potential, you have been controlled to such an extent that that potential has been denied its own existence. Most people use only 3 or 4 percent of their capabilities. Those who are more advanced may use 12 to 15 percent of their capabilities. Where does that leave most people? Where is the other 80 or 90 percent? What can that 90 percent of capabilities do? That 90 percent is awakening now, and the ancient eyes are going to begin to remember and see what the self is capable of being. When the ancient eyes are open, and you recognize your true potential, you will stop arguing with yourselves. You will stop arguing for limitation and will begin to move beyond the things that you insist on using to hold yourselves back.

In ancient Egypt, it took many lifetimes for the initiates trained in the priesthoods to completely open their eyes to other realities. They were trained to reincarnate into certain families and to remember who they were. Mothers and fathers understood who they would be birthing because they would dream of it. They would know who was coming into their bodies before they even moved into conception. The eyes were much more open then, and could see into many different realities. They were called the eyes of Horus because they could look into many different worlds—the world of waking and the world of sleeping, the world of death and the world of dreaming.

You who are wanting to open your ancient eyes and who are the masters awakening have experienced training in many other lifetimes. It is now your time to integrate this training into a body and into a system that has nothing to do with temple life—into something that is not waiting to give you a place for your abilities. You are renegades, so your society is not waiting for you to bring your gifts forward as it was in ancient Egypt. There is no place to put these talents to work within officialdom, no sect within society. This is not how you are living yet. So you will go at the pace that the body and soul and mind deem appropriate for the use of your talents.

Do not chastise yourself for not accelerating at the rate that your ego deems appropriate. The ego has eyes that see one part of yourself. The soul, or the eyes of Horus that look through you, has a completely different vision of what is appropriate. Knowing your needs, your constitution, and your blueprint, you will operate at a pace that will keep you intact. Mental institutions are filled with people who opened the ancient eyes and couldn't make sense of it or figure it out; they cannot find their home station. Without a place to plug into, the delicate balance of the nervous system is upset.

You are rapidly developing your nervous systems, and there are ways to recognize it. Every once in a while, you are able to catch the pulsation that takes you out of physical reality as you know it—out of the frequency that is third-dimensional identity. You are then able to move into another vibration and see, feel, and recognize that something out of the ordinary—something extraordinary—is going on. It is usually then that denial comes in, because if the logical mind can't explain what is happening or get a grip on it, you deny the experience or block the memory of it.

It is best if you stay in your intuition—if you rely on what you *feel* and, even though it may not make logical sense, operate with trust. Impatience is a trap for many of you because you feel you need to move somewhere. Don't deny the virtues of the turtle who moves very slowly, stops to go inside and contemplate, is close to the ground, and sees very well.

When you desire an acceleration in this opening of the ancient eyes, state your commitment. *Thought is. Thought creates.* If your thought is that you wish to move into an acceleration with the greatest growth and ability, that is what you will do. *When you doubt*, that doubt is a thought, too, and it will also create itself. When doubt occurs, it stops the expansion process because you deny the subtlety of what is coming to you.

You are in the decade that we have labeled "the unnamed decade": the 1990s. It is during this time that all the great events are going to begin to occur upon Earth. Many events have already been occurring, but they have been sequestered away in little compartmentalizations of officialdom. Officialdom is now outgrowing its own outfit and can no longer fit within its boundaries because it does not hold reality as it truly is evolving.

Those of you who are ancients—who are the masters awakening—as you awaken, we want you to be able to see out of the ancient eyes and to awaken something that you know, something that you *remember*, something that is deep inside. You are going to need to trust yourself and rely upon yourself. You need to be able to see, to *understand what you are seeing*, and to translate the grander vision for others. You will come to an understanding or a vast implosion of consciousness that will move you to know who you have always been.

It is up to you and only you to undo the locks and allow yourselves to go forward. We have spoken about your beliefs and the importance of thought. We emphasize over and over again that *you are a result of thought*, that *thought is*, and that this is the essence of understanding, manipulating, and working within your world. When you begin to take this process from the intellect and put it inside the body, and when you begin to commit to live your life this way, then the ancient eyes will really begin to see.

As you begin to view your soul's history, your identity in this particular body—the "I"—may seem to be very insignificant. You had a magnificent essence expressed on this planet in very ancient times, and there is so much more going on than you can presently perceive. It is as if existence is a book three feet thick and you are on the first couple of pages on this planet with the awakening of the New Age. You are going to go through this whole book in your lifetimes.

As you compute all of this information, the story will flood your consciousness as you begin to drop the boundaries of where you think you and civilization existed and came from. As you begin to disassemble your identity, cherish, honor, and love the variety of identities that are you, and do not feel that any of them are insignificant. Honor each one, whether you are picking strawberries in the fields or looking for cigarette butts on the street corners. Allow the aspect of self that carries the primordial fire to express itself through you. You can still be the "I" when it is appropriate to be the "I." Then, when the vastness of energy wishes to utilize your physical vehicle as part of the plan to effect reality, the "I" is not annihilated. Instead, the "I" is incorporated: *this is becoming multidimensional. This is being able to move.*

You each know that you are here in a time sequence that is quite profound. The age that has been written about, whispered about, and spoken about is upon you. It is the age when humanity physically mutates before your eyes and literally turns into something that it was not a short time before. What do human beings turn into? It is quite simple: human beings turn into multidimensional beings.

This is a big word and a big concept. However, it is something that will be as familiar to you as tying your own shoes. Multidimensional humans are humans that consciously exist in many different places all at once. Humans are mutating or evolving into beings with the ability to flip from one station to another and to understand the grandness of who they are—that they do not end where their skin ends. Human beings do not end where the aura or etheric body ends; they exist in many different realities.

This is the age of the multidimensional self: the self who can move with awareness in many different realities; the self who can eventually bilocate and disappear; the self who can move into fourth-dimensional consciousness—the *perceiver,* not the thinker. It is the age of the self who understands that the thinking portion of the self is very important but that it is not to be the CEO of the physical body; it is to be an advisor.

Intuition is the avenue that you are now being guided to cultivate to bring about a marriage of consciousness. It is the marriage of the male aspect, which is logical, with the female aspect, which is feeling. It involves bringing them together to become one.

It is time to get moving. You are at a very crucial point, and it is time for a huge change, a huge leap, a giving up, a releasing, and a letting go. It is time to completely allow light and spirit to move you throughout your existence, and time to let yourself become one with the multidimensional aspects of self and portions of self that you have no idea exist. These aspects of self really *do* exist. They are connected to you and are using you, the standard bearer of your soul, as the vehicle of movement for light in this universe at this time.

Those within our group who plotted the probabilities of Prime Creator were correct in much of their time travel and anticipation. Indeed, Prime Creator is sending a change of vibration to this area of existence, this free-will zone of consciousness. The action is taking place here on Earth now. It is starting here, at this corner of your galaxy, on the fringes, at this end of the universe.

This is a vast experiment, and it is with great excitement and great longing that each of you came to participate in it. Have courage. We cannot emphasize that enough: *have courage.* Follow your inner guidance and trust yourselves. Call energy into your physical bodies and utilize it. Defy the laws of humanity, because that is what you came here to do. You are renegades, and we are renegades as well.

There are those who cannot travel this route of consciousness, and that is fine. It is not an easy route that we move your consciousness through. The route will give you rewards that your soul is after, even though the rewards may come through battles. You are bushwhacking through consciousness, and you will come to a place where the vistas are grand and you have completely new options about where to go both on and off this planet. Those who are involved with you will discover that they have new options as well. All of the consciousnesses drawn to this planet at this time will begin a spark of evolution that will change the universal structure. *Think big.* Think really big and go for it.

Who are these multidimensional selves? Many times you have been led to believe that there are other portions of yourself that are much more together than you are and that know much more than you do. To some extent that was true, and to some extent it is still true. However, you will find that in being the standard bearer of your soul, you will begin to activate data that is stored inside of your body that carries your whole history. How will you know when these other aspects of self begin to show themselves? This can be very subtle, or it can be like being hit over the head with a two-by-four. It simply depends on the self. You may be sitting one day and find all of a sudden that upon blinking your eyes you are sitting in a different room. That is getting hit over the head with a two-by-four. More subtly, you may be walking down the street looking at a window display when suddenly a mannequin or picture or word triggers something inside of you; for a moment, you drift off and get a clear image of a simultaneous identity of yours—existing at the same time as you.

You will begin to discover aspects of yourself that exist nonphysically, or parts of self that exist as beings working in space who are truly space creatures. The soul is going to wake up. It will know every aspect of itself, and every aspect of the soul's self will know of all of itself at once.

You will be aware of all realities at once as you learn to ride the vibrational rate and become fourth dimensional. You will develop this ability by first balancing three or four realities, then five or six, and so on. You are awakening Prime Creator's abilities and will become *your* Prime Creator. Your Prime Creator's goal in creating this universe and all other universes was to develop itself to such an extent and have so many multidimensional channels of data open that it—whose consciousness is in all things you know—could become aware of itself in all things, aware of every event that all things are involved in, and compute this and not go insane.

You are evolving that ability in yourselves. Basically, the part that you are presently going through is the toughest part because you are doubting and wondering if it is really real. The body says one thing and the mind says another. The body says one thing and society says another. The knowing is growing, and it is a knowing of what is awakening inside of you.

You must be committed all of the time. When these gifts and abilities begin to be firsthand experiences for you, you must learn to work with them no matter what. Begin to know that you are divinely guided and that all events are drawn to you for your upliftment no matter what kind of upheaval they seem to produce in your life. Ultimately, these events will make you richer. The present situation is like someone dumping barrels full of gold in your back yard and you saying, "Gosh darn it, the gold is wrecking the grass." You think the lawn isn't as beautiful as it used to be because all of that gold is being dumped there.

Whenever you get an experience, learn to participate in it; be a full participant in your physical body. Enjoy it, have a good time with it, and learn how to simultaneously observe your experience, the impact of your experience, the affect your experience has on other people and yourself, and the results you get from all of your experiences. Then, whenever something of an extraordinary nature comes into being, you can say to yourself, "Oh, goody, goody—here it is again. What can I learn from this?"

When you are not having these experiences, begin to fantasize, to take charge of your life, and to *act as* if you can command or move one of these experiences the next time it sneaks up on you. You can do this the same way you may have learned to come awake in a dream and command that you not be chased by boogie men or to make the bell ring when you are just about to get an "F." You must, as individuals and as a species, cultivate this kind of belief or intention over all experiences of life.

There is a convergence of your selves about to occur on this planet. The selves that you are going to meet are coming from all over the universe. There are selves that petrify you when you think about them and selves that you could die of a heart attack looking at. *They are selves that are you.*

Earth is going through an initiation at this time. You are going through an initiation because you are part of Earth, and you cannot separate yourself from this system. Earth is transforming itself and intending to act as a domino for your solar system.

It is intending to merge multiple worlds into one, to be grounded enough to allow all those worlds to exist, and to translate the experience. This is what Earth is up to. So, of course, you all must be up to the same thing.

The 3-D world is headed for a collision of dimensions—not a collision of worlds, a collision of dimensions. Many dimensions are going to come crashing into each other. Some of these dimensions may seem horrifying and very frightening. The test, the initiation—and initiation always means to move through another reality to conquer it and transmute it—is to be faced with these energies and entities that seemingly are of incredible darkness and to understand that they are coming to merge with you because they *are* you. They are part of your multidimensional self, and you are the standard bearer, and *you are light*. Dark will come to light. Be very clear when you deal with these things. If you are hesitating about something, do not do it. Be clear.

We define light as the promoting, dispensing, and sharing of information. Dark is the controlling and withholding of information. Think about this and feel it. You have come onto this planet with a coded blueprint to carry light and to bring about a huge planetary transformation. You have come to be the standard bearer of your soul, the portion of your soul that is going to lead. That portion of your soul says, "I set the pace here, and the pace is light and information; no more being in the dark."

Have you ever thought that there are portions of yourself that are in the dark that don't know how to find the light except through you? They want the light as well. They want solutions and answers. What you may feel is not necessarily the intent of the dark force but the emotional makeup of the dark force—the fear that vibrates out of lack of information. Portions of yourself that are uninformed are going to come to you to be informed. How do you inform them? You shed light; you share light. You say, "I intend for all of my other selves to come along on this journey and for them to get light as well." It is quite simple.

The battle between light and dark doesn't really serve you.

It is part of the separation story that keeps you confused. In actuality, there are simply aspects of individual souls taking different guises in conflict with themselves. You are battling yourself. The battle of light and dark and good and evil is only between portions of yourself. These portions are multidimensional extensions or reincarnations of the same collective of energies that you are a part of as an individual. Because you don't understand something, you fear it. As separated forms of consciousness that are part of Prime Creator's game, you are in a universe that is made up of dualities. Prime Creator brought this universe into being with the components of free will so that free will could lead to chaos and then to a realignment of energy and a realization of the Creator within all things.

With free will, all things are allowed and oppositions occur. These oppositions split off of the self just as the Prime Creator is in all things and allows all things. The things you meet that you fear are *you*. So when you focus on the story of good and evil and want to figure it out, all you need to realize is that you are playing ball with another aspect of yourself that allows you to play ball from your point of view.

So-called evil serves a great purpose. You just judge it because it seems bad. As members of the Family of Light, when you exist in other places, you move into various aspects of yourself and play the parts to perfection. When you came here, you entered the density of the planet and worked with the double helix, which is barely functioning, so you forgot many things. Now, as you come awake and realize what you can become, you are leading yourselves toward the realization that *you* are your enemy.

As members of the Family of Light, you have access to a tremendous amount of understanding that others do not have. You came in with it, you are being reminded of it, and you are now learning it and accepting it. Part of your task is to allow yourself to merge with your selves that seemingly are your enemies and are separated from you. These selves are within all varieties of existence. The task is also for you to carry the frequency of love, which is the frequency of creation, and light, which is the frequency of information, throughout the collection of your soul. You have come together as a soul to gather experience and enrich Prime Creator. As you separate, you go off and act with free will however you choose, without judgment, so that you can gather the proper information and bring you to wholeness.

This good-and-evil thing is something that can entrap you if you do not get beyond it. You are a collection of an incredible wealth of personalities who incarnate in many different systems of reality. As members of the Family of Light, you come into this reality to bring information, and you do so in many different systems. There are versions of yourself that are doing the same thing within the communities of lizards, insect beings, or bird beings. *You are a collection of personalities.* As members of the Family of Light, the reincarnational experience of yourself includes nonhuman forms.

A characteristic that members of the Family of Light have in common with one another is their participation in many versions of sentient or composite reality. Many of the forms that you have chosen to incarnate within would look very foreign and be very frightening to you, yet this is how you have evolved your soul. You do not incarnate in only one species; you are travelers. As you are in disguise as humans, you may be in disguise as lizards or something else. You do this so that you can unite yourself to understanding the essence of Prime Creator through a variety of species that seemingly have nothing in common.

As members of the Family of Light, you know the inside scoop. You come as ambassadors to make realities merge and become more informed within themselves so that everyone involved can release fear and become uninhibited. Part of your job is to meet these other selves, to merge with them, and to feel what this is like. Ideally, you will become multidimensional travelers and will be able to take the force from your body. You may be working in the field, perhaps gardening or chatting with someone or picking strawberries, and something strikes you—a sound. You excuse yourself and say, "I am being called. I will return later." You go and sit and allow your current Earth personality to depart. With conscious awareness, you then take that personality to where it is needed to add to the Family of Light's capability in that reality. *You will know it.*

You will all become multidimensional players. You will think nothing of it when one of you excuses yourself from the others when you hear the tone and are called. You will travel with conscious awareness, and entertainment will come from the self. You will not seek to read books or listen to tapes or go to movies, for you will be living those things. As you bring the abilities of the Family of Light to this planet, others are not going to want you to be here, because you will not fit with their gods.

Not everyone wants to be free. You, as members of the Family of Light, are going to create a new Earth that is going to be free. Those who do not wish to be free will have their Earth as well. There will be a splitting and a time of separation. Members of the Family of Light know that there is no need to force anything. You are simply to work together in harmony, to support one another, and to seek one another out so that you feel comfort in what you do because some of the things that you do will be very outrageous.

Each of you volunteered to come here at this time to carry a frequency. At this time, that frequency is light, but eventually you will learn how to carry the frequency of love. The large majority of you have no idea what the love frequency can be. You talk about love and light, yet you do not comprehend the ramifications and the true meanings of them. Light is information; love is creation. You must become informed before you can create. Do you understand this?

As you grow and come to these higher realms of recognition, you will break through what feels like cement blocks—layers of yourself that have held you down. Think of the frequency that has limited the human experiment as a radio station. The human experiment has had one radio station on for

300,000 years. Same old tunes! The human experiment was unable to turn the dial and hear a different band, so the same frequency was broadcast. This created a quarantine—a sealing off of this planet.

The creative cosmic rays sent by Prime Creator and the Original Planners pierce through this frequency shield. They bombard Earth. However, they must have someone to receive them. Without a receptacle, these creative cosmic rays would create chaos and confusion. You, as members of the Family of Light, come into this system to receive these rays of knowledge. You then disseminate the knowledge, the new lifestyle, and the new frequency to the rest of the population to alter the entire planet.

As members of the Family of Light, you are here to anchor frequency and allow the mutation process to happen inside of your bodies so that you can make it available to the planet. You live this process, then you broadcast it to the planet. What does that mean? It means that eventually your reality is going to change and that how you deal with reality will change. You will stop being you, as you know you, and will become more connected with all of the other yous who are looking to make the same leap in consciousness as *this* you!

This process involves meeting and merging and using the multidimensional self. As you reach higher knowledge, you realize you are not alone and that there are multitudes of selves; you are challenged to understand this. There is no reaching higher knowledge without going through the multidimensional self. This means coming into full realization and experiencing, meeting, and merging with a collective of intelligence existing in the ever-expanding now, beyond space and time.

Believe us when we say that you, as members of the Family of Light, made a vast study of the historical manipulation that has been going on on this planet, just as anyone sent on assignment would be trained for a long period of time before they were sent out into the field. Each of you has been trained, and you have the knowledge inside you. Our part is to hit key chords and play your consciousness into activity so you can go ahead and make the tune or song or dance you are prepared for. Your knowledge is inside of you, and as you agree to discover it, it will awaken on deeper and deeper levels. You will become very self-sufficient, those of you who agree to this. You will also become incredibly knowledgeable, those of you who do not stop because you are frightened.

We will say to you very honestly that fear will always play a part in your evolutionary process, so get used to it. Do not feel that fear is bad. When you succumb to your fears and allow yourself to buy into them, then you must cycle through them and experience all you feel so that you can overcome them. Begin to say, "I will transmute this fear. I will understand that it is part of the plan. I will understand that it can serve me." Remember, your power and your ability to create reality through your will ends where your fear begins. And we will tell you—life is meeting fear. Begin to look at the events of your life and how you create them. Understand that you always create them to serve you. You are trained for this. You are coded for this.

EIGHT

Outside the Ultimate Tyranny

The ultimate tyranny in a society is not control by martial law. It is control by the psychological manipulation of consciousness, through which reality is defined so that those who exist within it do not even realize that they are in prison. They do not even realize that there is something outside of where they exist. We represent what is outside of what you have been taught exists. It is where you sometimes venture and where we want you to dwell; it is outside of where society has told you you can live.

You have been controlled like sheep in a pen by those who think they own you—from the government to the World Management Team to those in space. You have been deprived of knowledge by frequency control. Think of frequency as individual broadcasting and receiving through which you dial into the station of your choice. It is the broadcasting of carrier waves of intelligence. The range of frequency is unlimited, and the range of intelligent matter transmitted is unlimited.

Frequency control limits the number of stations you can tune into. As members of the Family of Light, you must anchor new frequencies through static chaos and bring them into the physical realm. The range of accessibility on this planet to a variety of frequencies has been very minimal for a long time because of many things that you most desperately need to become aware of. As you learn about your own personal history and discover patterns of ineffectual behavior that you must break and change, the planet pulses through its own patterns of behavior. You are about to repeat history as a planet in a most dramatic way.

You have come to alter and remove the frequency of limitation and to bring in the frequency of information. When you are informed, you move beyond the need to be in fear. When you feel uninformed and out of control, you do not understand the bigger picture. Each of you came to awaken something inside yourself, inside the coding of your being—the DNA—and you are responding to it. This is why you are on a search in all directions of your life.

You and multitudes of others have begun the mutation process on the planet. As you mutate electromagnetically, you alter your frequency or the tune that you broadcast. You will eventually outgrow the frequency that holds you down and continually blasts you with chaos and confusion. Eventually, when you alter, carry, and maintain your own frequency, you will vibrate differently and thus affect everyone around you. They will feel the availability of this frequency alteration, which will then move like a wave around the planet. As the planet accepts this new frequency that you have worked very hard to obtain, those at the end of the domino chain will receive it. This new frequency is called knowledge, light, and information. It is called being taken out of bondage. You are being taken out of disinformation and misinformation and you are becoming informed; you are coming into light.

As each of you has been assigned to become informed and to bring about a frequency alteration on this planet, you must learn to become Keepers of Frequency. You must rise to a certain place of knowledge and consistently stay there. You must become in command of your body so that you can will it into stillness or into activity. You must be able to go inside yourself and heal what needs to be healed emotionally and physically. You must begin to part the jungle of self and find the clearing so that you can show others the way. Sometimes you will show others the way not by speaking to them, but just by maintaining, living, and working on your own frequency and having the courage to do this.

As systems busters and potential Keepers of Frequency, you will obviously go into the areas where your specialities are most needed. Many of the beings who have incarnated as members of the Family of Light came to the United States because this is the land where you can make the most progress. This also happens to be a land where denial is pervasive. You believe that you live in the land of the free and the home of the brave, yet you live in the most controlled experimental society on the planet. The tyranny that has been set up here is rather interesting, because it is a tyranny without walls. As a country and a collective consciousness, the United States still has not reached an awareness that something is not right. The environment of the United States is actually much more controlled than that of the former Soviet Union, where the control was obvious.

Because everyone is so frightened of giving up the system in the United States, they are going to be *forced* to give it up. The system is corrupt, it does not work, it does not honor life, and it does not honor Earth. That is the bottom line. If something does not honor life and does not honor Earth, you can bet it is going to fall, and it is going to fall big-time.

Consciousness must change. This is part of the Divine Plan, and this opportunity and setup are not going to be missed. There has been an overinvolvement in the material world and a complete lack of understanding of the nonphysical world that exists all around you, so there will be a reprioritizing of what comes first in life. People will stand up, once they have lost everything, who had never thought of standing up when they owned everything. People will awaken to the incredible potential of themselves.

In the next few years, a connectedness and communal cooperation will begin to run through this country so that you will stop separating yourselves with respect to political ideology. That separation was designed. Whenever a people are separated, and they focus on what they do not have in common or label themselves different from others, it is a perfect disguise to keep them from discovering what they do have in common. This separation keeps people from banding together and becoming very strong.

Much of the political maneuvering going on, particularly in the United States, is purposely designed to separate you. Look at the New Age. Do you see how the New Age is separated? All kinds of things are said to keep you from discovering what you have in common. When people discover this, they will begin to get angry. As more and more of the methods of control and separation are revealed to you, the anger will build in the United States. Events will occur that may look as if the country is falling apart, yet they will serve the purpose of bringing people together. A new pride and a new sense of integrity will come about, because this is what is designed for the times.

The material realm is one area that everyone relates to. Life in the United States translates into how much money you have in your pocket and how much money the government wants out of what you have in your pocket. Taxes will be the issue that will create both the greatest amount of havoc in the United States and the greatest amount of unification, because you all have taxes in common. You may not worship the same God, but you all pay taxes.

In a clever move, the Middle East crisis allowed the government to have what it wanted without going through the problem of asking your permission for a tax raise on gasoline. You see how clever these things are? With a few more taxes piled on top of one another, people will begin to examine the quality of their lives. You will see a lot of anger in this country, because many people will feel powerless. Anger is one of the first emotions that will occur when people finally understand the manipulation that has been going on and begin to get in touch with their feelings.

Modern technology is one of the biggest weapons of frequency control. You have been sold devices for entertainment and convenience, and they are all involved with frequency control. We recommend strongly that you get rid of your television sets. They are the primary tool used to manipulate your consciousness on a day-to-day basis. This experiment is so finely tuned that you respond subliminally to disease via the television. So there is an entire generation that is killing itself by watching television—and supporting the medical society while they are doing it.

Sometimes liberating information is broadcast—perhaps even a New Age show. However, you may watch such a television show about how uplifted and unlimited you can be, while subliminally you are being hit with a frequency that keeps you from original thinking. This subliminal keeps you immobilized and holds you in a "survive, arrive, be-on-time, be-silent, go-to-work" society. Television also promotes inactivity and a sedentary, obese life. Look around you. *Wake up, humans!*

Most of the subliminals on television are done through technology that was developed in conjunction with off-planetary beings. The use of subliminals to upset human consciousness has become a worldwide program. If you think about the houses that have two, three, and four televisions in them, you must agree that this has been a very successful marketing program. Some people who know about the subliminals on television feel that they are immune to them. However, the effects of television are so permeating that no matter how clear you say you are going to be, you cannot counterbalance what the technology is presently doing to your vibrational frequency.

We have said that there are entities who feed off your emotional bodies. Think about what a clever tool television is for them. All over the world, billions of humans are emitting emotional juices into the atmosphere based upon what they are watching on the tube. They don't have to have too many wars anymore to get you all riled up—they can simply make movies!

People who need to watch television are not tapping into the wealth of information within their minds and immediately accessible all around them. As a matter of fact, if you really want to evolve, do not read your newspapers, do not listen to the radio, and do not watch television. If you are able to be media free for periods of time, and you disengage yourself from the frequency of chaos and anxiety and stress and hustle-bustle and temptations of all kinds that you don't need, you begin to get clear. You begin to listen to what is going on inside of yourself and to live of the world and not necessarily be lost in it. You become clear. We cannot emphasize this enough!

Electronics also jam your frequency. Even when they are not specifically designed to jam your frequency, sometimes there is incompatibility between the electronic frequency of something and yourself. Plus, as we said, many of them are designed to create static so that you will always stay at a certain vibratory rate, turning you into safe, harmless, inactive, productive cattle.

What about computers? The second most predominant piece of hardware in the United States is the computer. How many of you go to work on computers and end up getting headaches, particularly when you work for large corporations and are hooked up to their mainframe? Large companies are into aspects of mind control; they use your minds to generate energy to achieve something for themselves. Personal computers are not as potent and powerful.

Some new inventions are going to surface in the nineties—very underground inventions, because they will never be given patents to be promoted in the marketplace. There will be a whole underground economy based upon barter, in which certain inventions will be traded between people. There will be technologies that can counteract much of the frequency control: these technologies can change the quality of your air and water, and they can eliminate and seal off your home so that you are an integral of energy and nothing can bombard you. There are technologies that do phenomenal things. Do you understand how technology has been used against you? It has not been used *for* you. Television is not necessarily bad in itself, but it has been put to ill purpose. There is nothing wrong with technology. *It is how technology is being used* that is the bottom line. That is the difference.

The education system is another area where you are controlled. Most of what you are taught is malarkey. You work hard, take loans out, and pay money to learn something that is antiquated before you even set foot in the door, particularly in the realms of scientific, mathematical, psychological, and medical exploration.

What do you do when you live in a society that rewards you for degrees? You begin by saying, "I believe that I formulate my world. I believe that I do not need these credentials to define my existence. I can be unique unto myself, sovereign unto myself." Come up with a method or way to explore the world without degrees. Education is actually the pursuit of knowledge, and knowledge can come from a walk in the desert. It does not have to come from flipping pages in a book. It is not harmful to explore a little bit of schooling, but don't buy into the idea that what you are being taught is correct.

You are controlled and separated by issues that strike at the core of your emotions. The abortion/pro-life issue is not a global issue, it is a national issue. Sometimes it does look as if innocent victims are trampled or stampeded by events that seemingly have nothing to do with them. Of course, that is what you have been taught—that you are powerless and can only be saved by the mood of the gods, which has never been the case. Those who find their lives taken by accident or violence *select it*.

The pro-life/abortion issue has been purposely orchestrated in the United States by different factions within the government to create a lack of harmony. Divide and conquer, and you own the people. Allow the people choice, freedom, and the ability to continuously improve their lives, and you cannot own them. Whenever people oppose people, those in control benefit, even down to the issue over abortion.

How do they benefit? They keep women from uniting with each other and men from uniting with each other here in the United States. They keep people in fear. They convince you, by continuously putting these issues before you, that a woman has no control over the birthing process in her body. You don't need abortion: you never need to get pregnant in the first place if you don't desire it. How? *By will.* A woman can say to herself, "I am not prepared at this time for a child." Or, alternately, "I am in receptivity of a child." When you own yourself, you will not need permission from the government about what you can do with your own body.

Violence on the streets of major cities is another subtle means of control. The big cities in the United States—Los Angeles, New York City, Washington, D.C., and so on—are energy buckets, or holes, where energy comes into the North American continent—or has up until now. There has been an increase in violence in these cities because it is known that if unrest can be kept brewing and reported, it can be a likely vehicle for manipulating the entire nation. These things are purposely set into motion on the physical level and assisted on the etheric level because the more fear that is generated the more those in charge can feed on it.

When a woman goes out with her family and is assaulted, and her young son, a seemingly innocent victim, fights the assailants and goes down by knife and dies totally unexpectedly on his vacation, the fear that is promoted throughout multitudes of people feeds many. The fear that the war in the Middle East brought about was phenomenal.

You have been raped of your life force. If there is anything that you as members of the human species have in common it is that you have been raped for your emotions. Others have played your emotions as though they were instruments, and they have never let you know the power you have with your emotions.

Always this whole story comes back to emotions. Emotions are like tickets that can get you places and plug you in. You are incredibly rich. If you would only realize how wealthy you are with your emotions. The lower vibratory beings, if we may be so bold as to call them that, exist off emotions in a very small range of frequency—emotions that are based on fear, chaos, and violence.

The ability to use the human will over the human mind is your ultimate resource. This ability to master the body according to your will is exactly what the people in charge of the planet do not want you to figure out. As more of you become sovereign and in charge of your own frequency, those who do not want the new frequency here will bring an opposite frequency to create chaos, confusion, and polarity. Always, whenever a society is on the verge of a huge leap or change, there are diametrically opposed activities.

Always look at an issue from the perspective of the bigger picture so that you have neutrality with it, for the picture gets bigger and bigger all the time. The planet is headed for a major confrontation with certain entities. We are simply pointing this out; we are not here to promote fear. Fear is what the other team wants you to feel. We want you to understand that *you can change anything you want to change.* This is going to be a game of numbers in the future, because you will work together to bring yourselves to a place of empowerment.

We are asking humans to come into full function as members of the Family of Light by imaging and energizing the pillar of light and pulling it inside the body. Command it. Make it your intention every day to operate with a cordon of light, for light frequency connects you and fills you with protection and information. Feel it move into the base of your spine, down your body, and into the Earth, as well as coming out of your solar-plexus area like a fountain and forming a golden shield of light around you. As you use the solar-plexus area to determine what is going on, you will learn *discernment through feeling.*

Earth's owners have not wanted humans to understand that their feelings and emotions are like a crop, such as wheat, that can be harvested. If you are in charge of your own harvest, then others cannot take advantage of you and use you unless you decree it. When you operate with a certain frequency and sovereignty, those who wish to control you are not interested in you. They want a fearful, chaotic frequency, which is what nourishes them. Fear and chaos have predominated on this planet because these entities have stirred them up. They have divided and conquered everywhere to create that frequency. When you operate in peace and love and with information, you alter the structure of this place drastically: you bring choice of frequency back to this planet.

NINE

Profound New Boundaries

Since you are a frequency-controlled society, the ability of humanity to create technologies has been limited. In a less controlled society that has greater outreach or travel capabilities through space and greater interchange between systems, technological advances are quite astounding and uplifting. Many gifts and influences from outside this planet have been hushed up. Some information has, of course, been given to the planet in many different ways, and the resulting technologies have brought about great changes in lifestyle.

One of the changes in lifestyle that occurred during this century was the introduction of movies. A whole new way of influencing thought was brought to the planet by the film industry. Just as there is a movie industry on this planet, there are those in space who have a holographic industry. They make holographic inserts—dramas that look just like they are real—and insert them through portals into your reality. Since these space beings have been around for hundreds of thousands of years, and humanity's frequencies have been controlled, it is quite easy to hoodwink human beings.

Holographic inserts have been used on Earth to manipulate and control consciousness and to change the story of information to one of disinformation—one of a limited amount of knowledge. As we see it, those who use the holographic inserts are not always after bringing light or information or upliftment to people. They have ulterior motives, although they may pass them off as light.

Holographic experiences, especially viewings in the sky, are set up to influence a large group of people at once. Many, though not all, UFO sightings have been holographic inserts. There have been holographic inserts of one individual, designed in many fashions, projected simultaneously in many different cultures. That is why some of Earth's religious stories are parallel from one corner of the world to another when there was no physical contact.

Holographic inserts look exactly like 3-D reality. They are creations of events manufactured and inserted in your reality to look as if they are part of a sequential action. They are used to influence the minds of observers, and they are very difficult to recognize. You will have plenty of practice in the next number of years when—in the Middle East and other areas around this planet—a lot of extraterrestrial activities come into full force and begin to be published. Some of the grand events will be very legitimate, and some of them will be inserts designed to move the consciousness of humanity toward the one world order to be controlled.

Holographic inserts have energy fields and can be dowsed. Dowsing rods move differently in them because their energy fields are diverse and vibrate at an incredible rate. You can walk into them and participate in them. People may be part of them and swear they are real. But they are orchestrated events designed to influence the minds of humans. Holographic inserts are not done for information, they are done for control. They are simply an aspect of technology that exists.

Realities can be constructed and inserted just like movies. Movies, television, and so on are your version of creating reality. There are other, very evolved beings who cleverly create realities so "real" that you can't tell the difference. They are like beams. Just like spotlights are projected into the night, holographic inserts are projected onto this planet through portals. Tremendous energy is needed because the process involves the merging of dimensions. The technology does not exist in the third dimension, it exists in other dimensions, and they need the dimensional fusions.

What is the difference between dimensions? Why is one dimension important to another? Because each dimension has a different vibratory rate or way the molecules move. These holographic inserts need places where the dimensions are already merged because they need to play through the other dimensions in order to enter here.

Humanity has been blind and hoodwinked over and over again because of the unevolved helixes that information could not plug into. The Family of Light has come to change all of that. You are here to carry a new frequency on the planet and hold it in your bodies so the rest of the planet can begin to vibrate at the same frequency. That frequency is going to create disruption of the structures based on two-stranded DNA on this planet. It cannot help it; it is time to evolve. Earth is ready to go through whatever is necessary for that evolution.

Human beings must learn to read energies. They must learn to use more than the senses of their eyes, ears, nose, mouth, and so on to perceive reality. We have said that the eyes, ears, nose, mouth, and sense of touch are *deceivers of reality*. They lock reality in. You think you are perceiving reality with these senses when in actuality they limit your perceptions of reality. You have been trained since you were a child to rely on your eyes, ears, nose, mouth, and sense of touch to interpret experience. Now you are going to need to rely on other forms of sensing to determine experience. One of the forms you have discounted is feeling. Feeling—your knowing, intuitive, psychic self— has been jammed by frequency control on this planet so that none of you have been able to find it. If you found your own knowledge and your own way of intuiting, you could not be controlled.

How do you know what is controlled and what is not controlled? Part of your experience here is to learn that—to get into a little hot water and to know when to jump out. In the deepest core of your being, there is an integrity you can discover and begin to operate with. It is an integrity that honors life and honors yourself first and foremost as the life that you are in charge of. *You are in charge of you,* and it has been gifted and granted to you that you honor your light, your body, and your experience to the best of your ability.

As you begin to take good care of your integrity and to cultivate it and discover the miracle and potentials of it, you will discover that your body, which seemingly has been somewhat of a burden that you have been carting around, is really invaluable. It brings you untold wealth. With the physical body, you are millionaires. You must learn to use your feeling center and to activate and act on the information inside of you; you must learn to trust it.

You, as members of the Family of Light, are intending to merge dimensions. Your task is to pull other dimensions into this reality, to have your nervous system handle the different molecular fluctuations, and to be able to make it OK. You are learning to perceive through your feeling centers and to teach others how to do all that you can do. You are the way showers.

You will recognize holographic inserts by feeling. They won't *feel* right—something will feel fishy or strange. When holographic inserts are put into your reality, something is not right. As members of the Family of Light, your codings and filaments will not feel good if you are exposed to holographic inserts because they are used to control you rather than bring you to upliftment. They are used to ride your emotions to a certain point so others can feed off them and to bring you to a certain new level of operation.

These technologies will be used more in the next decade. That is why we say that humanity is in for a drastic awakening as far as what is really real. The boundaries of reality are quite profound.

We talked about the portal in the Middle East being a dimensional doorway or entryway onto the planet for certain energies to find civilization. Remember, when you leave a planetary sphere and go into space, once you traverse certain belts of consciousness you must find the proper portal to come back onto the planet in the precise time period or corridor of time that you are looking for. This is how systems are kept locked and intact, and how they are prevented from being raided and taken over. There are portals on the South American continent, the North American continent, Asia, China, and all over the globe. The huge portal that we are presently discussing is the portal in the Middle East. It is gigantic.

Many holographic inserts or dramas have been inserted through that portal to upset the minds and beliefs of the population. Since this portal is in the midst of crisis, it is a prime candidate for holographic inserts and also prime for a belief system to alter this chaotic world and get everyone to move in a different direction. Be aware of your feeling centers when these kinds of events begin to occur on this planet.

The Middle East is a portal where many dimensions meet and where entities from other dimensions can come onto this planet. It is a hot spot. In recent times, in the last forty or fifty thousand years, many civilizations have surfaced and many religious dramas have started in the Middle East. Because of the vortex, holographic inserts are easier to produce in that area, just like movies are easier to produce in California.

A potential holographic insert in this portal is the arrival of extraterrestrials from space. Or Christ returning. Or some god returning, or some savior, or some reason for everyone to begin to follow one way of thinking. At this time, as we see it, it is not of light. An example of a holographic insert that was put on the planet in the past to change the course of history is the crucifixion of Christ. The drama that was played out and passed on historically to you is not the reality that the Christed One came in to play. A *version* of this entity's life was molded and designed in a holographic entertainment movie, which was then inserted and played out as if it were real.

Christ came in as a committee of beings over a period of time. The story that you have been told is a dramatized, marketed version—a very controlled version of who this entity was and is. Part of the Christ drama you have been taught was a holographic insert. And part of what you will discover in the future about the Christed One has the potential of being another holographic insert. So be aware. Most people would say that we are sacrilegious and of the devil to say this. How can we question what the Bible says? How can we question all of these things? Because they were all said and done by patriarchal organizations that promoted themselves. That was all they were. They were utilized to bring back control of the energy on the planet.

In reality, the Christed One was sent as a systems buster, a member of the Family of Light, to bring light through the portal in the Middle East. This created a way for *many* to enter and seed a reality that would prepare the consciousness of humanity for the cycle that will terminate in approximately the next twenty years, depending upon how events proceed. The Christed One came not as one entity but as a number of entities, influencing people in humanity's dark hour, an hour when human beings were ready to understand their mysteries. One of the things that was not promoted to you in a very truthful way was that the Christed One was very well accepted. The kind of energy that the Christed beings brought to the planet was received very well.

There are a number of dramas going on with the Christ entity. There is the original blueprint: the plan of the Christed committee to come in, to spread light or information, and to show humans what the human body is capable of doing. Then there are the beings who said, "What are we going to do about this? This one is coming in our portal, and we want control over this portal. How are we going to be able to use this energy? It is a free-will universe, and we can do what we want." So they created a holographic insert of the drama of Christ being crucified to create fear and emotion out of someone else's intentions and to move consciousness in a way that was not originally intended at all. This means that in a free-will universe it is possible, particularly in portal areas, for one group of gods to raid another's story and insert their own version of it. At the time, perhaps, this does not affect many, although over time the impact of the holographic insert is eventually known.

We know this is frustrating for many of you. Yet what we are doing by sharing this information with you is getting you to move, feel, remember—and not *think* so much. This is not a process of logical thinking, it is a process of feeling. What is going on with your body? Ask yourself, "What is my identity? How can this be? Who am I within it?" Then you will begin to release more of who you are to yourself, and you will be able to figure out many things.

Do you understand why you have come here to bust the system? Do you understand how complex frequency control is? Do you understand how fine and thin reality is? Do you understand how available reality control is to the human species— if humans would harmonize with one another, and act as though they were all provided for, and believe and create through their minds?

We said some time ago that light is underestimated on this planet. Truly it is. If it became known how many individuals are gaining sovereignty over their thoughts and lives, and how many of them are broadcasting this sovereignty and living to teach it to others, those in charge would do something about it rather quickly. Light is underestimated, and it is a good thing, because light is going to liberate you all.

You have an exciting assignment—an enviable job—and you have all the help you are going to need to complete your task. There has been a tremendous influx of entities and mother ships on this planet that are now acting as intermediaries or perhaps literal transducers of energy. The beams of light that come to the planet come from old and ancient star systems that have been working with Earth for eons and eons. Many of them are simply numbered by your astronomers, while others have names you are familiar with—Sirius, Arcturus, Orion, the Pleiades, and so on. Beams of light are being caught by quite a number of mother ships surrounding Earth, filtered through an entirely different system, and then blasted onto the planet.

Many of you have implants inside of you to respond to this communication and to bypass psychotronic warfare and interference that would keep your frequencies jammed and prevent you from being able to receive this information. These implants are not negative. You were not abducted and probed to receive them against your will. They are etheric implants that you called to yourself as tools to receive off-planet energies. These implants are being activated now. Many of you are finding that you are feeling altered. At different times of the day, particularly when you are going to sleep, you are hearing a variety of tones or feeling a kind of electric vibration in your body.

When this information is beamed to you, your body must be able to receive it. In order for your body to receive it, it must be in a certain state. The information is like a current, and if your body cannot handle the current it moves into a state of discomfort. The people of Earth were programmed for this time, and there is no one incarnated upon the planet who can say that they made a mistake and did not know what was going to occur here. No one was born upon this planet without a mechanism inside of them that can be activated to tune into or turn on to the ability to house these frequencies.

We have encouraged many of you to move out of the logical mind because the logical mind will come into conflict with this information and electronic energy. In the next number of years, your understanding and vibration with the frequencies coming to you will be like turning on your own radio. You will have a direct telepathic link with mother ships broadcasting to you. There will come a time when you will never even think of going to a channeling session because you will have your own linkup with information. The wealth of information that will come to you will be of great reassurance; it will be broadcast to fill you in on what is happening.

As you become more trusting, you will be able to manifest before you a light entity who will come physically and begin to teach you. Channeling, or the process of bringing information through another being, will become completely archaic as each of you manifest your own literal being to teach you. In the meantime, we are here to teach you, to remind you of who you are, and to give you an idea of what you can draw to yourself. What we want more than anything else is to assist you, as members of the Family of Light, to succeed in liberating the humans. Focus on the dance of yourself. To what tune will you dance and to what ma-gic will you perform and to what heights will you be willing to push consciousness to give it a new definition of possibilities?

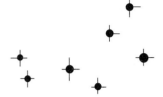

TEN

A New Paradigm of Light

Who are the Bringers of the Dawn, and what is their role? The Bringers of the Dawn are those who carry the rays of the sun and bring light and knowledge. They have an ancient organization, an ancient society, an ancient spiritual bonding that keeps them doing certain work within a certain star system. You are members of the Bringers of the Dawn; otherwise you would not be drawn to this book. The members of this elite organization come to Earth at different times to do their work. This occurs when a cycle has been set and events are perfect for them to allow the energy from the high cosmos and the energy from Earth to merge within their own beings.

The energies from the cosmos are always coming to Earth, and the energies from Earth are always lifting up toward the cosmos. Humanity creates the sacred bridge between Earth and sky, which some have called the rainbow bridge. The Bringers of the Dawn allow these energies to merge so that the dawn, or the light, is awakened within them. They then bring that dawn to civilizations. *This is who you are. This is what you are doing.* So are multitudes of others. You are the Bringers of the Dawn.

As Bringers of the Dawn, there is a certain stance that will facilitate the commitment you have made. This stance is one of *allowing* and moving out of self-indulgence and the discounting of your experiences. For the Bringers of the Dawn, each link makes up the whole, no matter how it is constructed, no matter what strength or weakness it has, and no matter how big or small its role. Strength or weakness or influence are not necessarily to be compared; they are simply the stance that consciousness, in its own dance of reality, chooses to focus upon.

We teach you about yourselves and assist you in unlocking what is inside of you, not what is outside of you. As Bringers of the Dawn, you are in your darkest hour before the dawn, when you may wonder if there is going to be a ray of light. Then, almost instantly, the light will begin to show from nowhere. Where will it come from? How will it change your thinking? How is existence as dark as it can be one moment, and then the next instant there is light? As Bringers of the Dawn, you *will* that light to dawn. You were trained for this; it is your forte.

You, the Bringers of the Dawn, also known as the Family of Light, agreed to go through the process of mutation to evolve yourselves into higher beings by intention and conscious agreement. You bring light back to the planet, bring about the new evolution of humanity, and make the cosmic evolutionary leap in awareness and intelligence possible by anchoring the frequency first inside your own bodies and living it.

The Family of Light comes from a central place of operation—a source within this universe that acts as a broadcast station. There are central suns within your galactic system and a central sun within this universe. The Mayans named this central sun Alcyone. Others know it by other names. The sun has light, and light has information. To make this very simplistic, members of the Family of Light come from a place that is the central storehouse of information for the universe.

You cycle or spiral out from this central sun and carry the information from it throughout the various systems in this universe; you plot, plan, and travel. You are very unique in this regard, and you know it. You know when you look at the population that you are very different. You love rabble-rousing, and you love to bust systems open. When something says, "No Trespassing," it is for everyone else and not for you. You go wherever anything is shut down so that you can open it up. You operate by separating yourselves into many multidimensional identities and then going into systems to change them.

You sometimes incarnate in these systems for hundreds of thousands of years in preparation for the time when you may be called on to bust the systems. You have a resume to back you. For example, you incarnate on Earth a number of times so that if the call goes out that Earth is going to be busted open and the paradigm is going to be shifted, you can say, "I have been there 247 times, in this many varieties, and once I was able to ascend my body. I did this, this, and this. If I go in for this game plan to bust the system, I am certain that I can refresh my memories, pull them up, defy the laws, and complete the assignment."

Sometimes it doesn't happen and the plan has to be aborted for some reason. That is a very frustrating experience for you. However, when all goes according to plan and you succeed in busting the system and creating a new paradigm of light, it is like a cosmic orgasm to you.

Members of the Bringers of the Dawn or the Family of Light work in teams. You don't go into systems alone. You need each other to do this work because you cannot hold the frequency by yourself. By going in as teams, you increase the odds of successfully carrying out the plan. You are like rays and light spirals of the central sun that are very intelligent, and you are guided by a great intelligence inside the central sun.

Light is a kingdom of consciousness, and it has a purpose in existence. The story we tell you today is a story that you can comprehend. Every time we speak to humans and you comprehend more, we give you more. We do not want you to think that light is more noble than anything else. Something in the essence of your soul connects you to this light source and drives you to this profession, but it does not make this profession better than any other profession. There are others who have different sources and spiral out with different intentions, and they make the ballgame possible. You are learning about this.

We remind you that Prime Creator creates it all, and it endows all things with itself. Just as you are seeking self-awareness, Prime Creator is mastering this as well. It seeks to be aware of itself within all things and to endow the things that it is within with awareness that Prime Creator is in them and aware of its existence. The awareness is like a mirror going back and forth between Prime Creator and all creations, down to the smallest little bug or ant that crawls on the ground. Just as Prime Creator is in light, it is also in so-called evil, knowing that "evil" also has a divine purpose.

Many kingdoms of consciousness exist. "Kingdoms of consciousness" are fancy words for a concept that we would like you to grasp. Within the kingdoms of consciousness, there is a likeness of energy, and there are many kinds of kingdoms of consciousness. The Family of Light comes from a particular kingdom of consciousness.

When your consciousness learns the laws of creation, manipulation, and management of reality, it is quite easy for you to manifest into any form you choose. For those of you who have activated your shamanistic and native cultural memories, you well know that part of the teachings of native cultures was how to go into various realities and change form. The shamans in certain cultures were revered for this. They carried genetic coding, and there were very few on the planet in relation to the entire population. They held the magic and mystery and kept the process alive. They were able to move in the forms of animals and various other shapes and guises. This was quite a profound science, indeed.

Because this science exists *on* the planet, of course, it also exists *off* the planet. Earth is a "happening" place right now, a hot spot. It is coded to start its own revolution—not necessarily just a revolution in the United States to change lifestyle, but a dimensional shift that is going to alter all of the space around Earth.

Many extraterrestrials who are curious about life forms know how to rearrange their molecular structures and come onto the planet in disguise as humans. In times of tumultuous change, when dimensions have the potential to merge and collide—as you are setting up here for Earth—there is a great gathering of energies that come to participate in the big show.

The big show happens on many levels, not just in 3-D. A chain reaction moves through all of the dimensions of existence and all of consciousness. Some beings beam themselves to Earth in disguise as humans, or they incarnate, picking an opportunity to get a ticket into this reality to be here for the event. Perhaps some of those you sense as not native to the planet and not here as systems busters are here to observe, to participate, and to understand so that they can take the information back to their own systems, which are always evolving.

There are intelligent creatures who are able to manifest as humans and play the role out to perfection; sometimes their memories are intact, and sometimes they have the veil down. It is not always easy for these beings to come here with full conscious memory of who they are elsewhere because of the frequency control. You will grow in your awareness over the next few years that you are members of the Family of Light in disguise as humans. Part of the planned evolution of the human species and the planned rearrangement of the human DNA is for each person to begin to open a memory bank and remember who they are.

In different dimensions of reality, there are, of course, different experiences and different laws. In 3-D, where you have been locked as a human species for so long, there is a limitation on what you can experience. The third dimension is designed to focus on one existing reality at a time. It is designed this way according to frequency and nerve pulsation and the rate that frequencies adjust the nerve pulsations within the body.

You are magnetically and biogenetically tuned and designed. The members of the Family of Light are *much more than human*. Characteristically, you are supreme achievers in the multidimensional realm. One applies for a position in the multidimensional realm as a member of the Family of Light.

As members of the Family of Light, you have incarnated on this planet to prepare yourselves to do your work. What is your work? Your work is quite simple: you carry frequency into systems that have limited light frequency, because light is information. This is not cold, computer-data information; it is information that is transmitted biologically through an electromagnetic send-out of consciousness. This is what you are experts in. If you were to have a business card printed up for yourselves when you are in full memory of your identity, it would say something like: "Renegade Member of Family of Light. Systems Buster. Available for altering systems of consciousness within the free-will universe. On call."

You go for it! This is what you do. This is an aspect of your identity that you all have in common, and you are here in the millions at this time. You are here primarily *to remember who you are*, to operate multidimensionally within the system, and to teach humans—the natives in this place that have been under frequency control for a long time—a new system. *You are disguised as humans.* As soon as you begin to realize this, you will extricate yourself from the human drama and the human dilemma of frequency control.

Before frequency control was instituted 300,000 years ago by the raiding group of creator gods, the native species was somewhat clever. They had a very evolved system of receiving information and could directly receive on the planet from space contacts. They also had many different ways of distributing knowledge as it was received. Distributing knowledge on the planet at this time is based on technology—something outside of yourself. It is another clever bill of goods you were sold as a means of control. A long time ago, communication on this planet occurred through contact with one another by the use of internal mechanisms, not by technology outside of yourself.

Most humans cannot grasp that their history goes back more than a few thousand years. You will learn, remember, and teach the planet that it has a history of millions of years. First, you will uncover and integrate the history of the planet for the past 300,000 years so that you can expand the picture of the human dilemma. Remember, the history is all inside of you, not outside of you. In your current technology, light-encoded filaments are being created outside of your body in symbolic form as a representation of the transmission of intelligence through fiber optics. The human species creates *outside* of itself what it must learn is *inside* of itself. It is part of the mastery of light.

When the great library of yourselves was put into chaos, there was a little bit of data left that kept the species controllable, operable, manageable, and yet functioning on its own, performing tasks and stimulating it as a life form and form of consciousness to produce a certain frequency: fear. This fear has been promoted for the past 300,000 years on this planet as a controlled substance in every version that you can think of.

When a human being resonates electromagnetically and broadcasts the frequency of fear, a transmission of consciousness is sent out. Where does that fear go? Where do your thoughts go? Where do your emotions go? We have already said that, collectively, consciousness forms food. As systems busters, you have come in to eradicate the food source, or to change the food source from one of fear and chaos. Those who are nourished by that food source will have to either change their diet or leave this planet. You are here to bring information, light, the comprehension that there is potential for change, and a food source that works in cooperation and resonates with light. This is what you are about and what it is your responsibility to achieve.

We understand that some of you are very puzzled about how to do this and how to bring about this state of impeccability in your own lives. One of the primary things we ask each of you to do from this moment forward is *to not base any of your future experiences on your past.* All of you love to drag the past in as an excuse for what might happen in the future. You are famous for it. But you must act as if you are newly beamed down, innocent as a babe, and ready to step forward into the circumstances of your daily life. As you awaken each morning and step forward each day, state with clarity what you intend to experience that day. If you are not doing this or cultivating the habit of doing it, then you had best get going! It is the way that reality is designed.

As we have said before, the big secret that has been kept from the human species is that *thought creates experience, and thought creates reality.* All reality is created by thought. It is all a subjective experience. But electromagnetically, you are being controlled in such a way as to create experiences within a certain spectrum of reality.

You who are members of the Family of Light are well traveled and well attuned to the possibility of bringing new frequencies in. You have come here to hold the new frequencies being beamed to you from space that are setting into motion a new pattern inside your bodies. As you begin to know that this is your purpose, you will begin to design your purpose consciously, to get clear about what you want, and to experience it, no matter what area it is in. This is an absolute.

Each of you likes drama in your own way. You get bored if you don't have "stuff" happening. This is why you formulated this plan—this raid. In actuality, this reality or world was set up by entities of the Family of Light a long time ago, before the reality was raided. As members of the Family of Light, you were the Original Planners. There were many rich funds of consciousness here that were free to become attached to and to utilize. When the entities of other families that you have come to call "dark" took over this planet, they did a very good job of keeping light out. Light is only as big as your paradigm can get at this time, but there are other teams and kingdoms of consciousness out there as well. For now, we will just work with light and dark. The dark team did a very good job of keeping light out for a long time. *However, that time is up!*

You are renegades of light, and you decided to come back and stage another raid of consciousness—millions of you at this time—because you knew in working with Prime Creator's energy that there was a high probability that everyone would achieve a great richness of consciousness. As you begin to pull this light into your bodies and onto the planet, many people who like drama may be affected. They may be pierced by light and have a reaction, because the more light you bring the faster it will spread. Light is definitely growing on the planet as you remember that you are the native species, working closely with the Original Planners, here to take back your world from the raiders.

ELEVEN

The Name of the Game

In order to survive in the times that are coming, it is imperative to move into the idea of thought manifestation or superconsciousness. Superconsciousness is only a word to you at this time. It is not a concept that is inside of you yet because you cannot conceive of being so in tune and filled with so much information. Yet, as you evolve, that is what you are moving toward. There are those who are very aware that this movement of consciousness could begin to sweep the planet, and they are banking on it not occurring. *It has already occurred.* We have come back into your past to assure you of this.

Thought comes first. Experience is always secondary. It is never the other way around—that you have the experience and then you base the thought around it. Always your experience is a direct reflection of what you are thinking.

Clarity and recognition of your own power are the bottom line. Your thoughts form your world *all of the time.* Not cafeteria style—*all of the time.* Because you are bombarded with so many frequency-control vibrations that attempt to keep you from being clear, you fluctuate. You must, as a species, make it your intention to stay very clear, to stay centered, and always to bring yourself into the moment. Stop living in the future or living in the past, and always live in your now. Say to yourself, "What do I want? I want to accelerate my personal evolution. I want Spirit to assist me in a greater capacity. I want my body to regenerate itself. I want to emanate health. I am willing to give up difficulty so that I can be a living example of what humanity can be." It is this line of thinking—this commanding from your being and calling out what you want with clarity—that brings you everything in acceleration.

Watch your patterns. If you find yourself denying that you created a portion of your experience, and you don't want to own it as your creation, simply look at it. Say, "Isn't this interesting—I do this all of the time. I don't want to own what I am creating. If I don't like it, I blame someone else. Let me see how long I will do this, and let me come up with a solution to develop a different pattern of behavior."

Don't judge yourself. Begin to say to yourself, "I will accept responsibility for all that I am involved in. I will accept responsibility for everything that happens to me. If I don't like what is happening to me, I will begin to ask myself why I create things that I don't like. Maybe it's to get my attention about something so that I can change what is really not working for me that I cannot see."

Always act as if there is an impeccable purpose to everything you do. Act as if your highest good and your highest opportunity involve working through every event you are involved in. Always act that way. If you are walking down the street and someone says, "I've got a gun in your back; let's have your purse," act as if you are being given an opportunity for your highest growth. You never know what the results are going to be if you begin to act this way. When you *act as if*, you act without knowing and without expectation. This is an attitude. If you all could have this attitude and act as if every event is designed to propel you further in your growth and awareness, then you might turn around and find that the person holding the gun in your back is a counterpart or portion of yourself. You might be able to heal something; you might be given an opportunity to do something you are afraid of.

Do not be afraid of what you create. *Trust what you create.* Trust that there is always something in it for you. Do not sweep your dramas under the rug as if they are dirty old horrible things and you never wish to see them again. Get finished with these dramas: stop cycling in them and being lost in them. However, understand that the drama you have had with your mother, your brother, your sister, your lover is something you may use twenty years later to come to a whole new realization. So let these life dramas be like a file for you. Finish them up, resolve them as best you can, create peace, accept your part in them, and then let them cycle back through your consciousness to teach you something. Let them be ongoing treasures of experience for yourself rather than hackles that you want to get past. Emotion is connected with these things, and remember, emotion can take you into other realms of activity.

Do you believe that you only create your reality in certain areas and that in other areas you are disempowered? Do you argue that you have no control over some areas of your life? Do you give up what is naturally yours because society tells you you cannot have it? You will find that events do not come out of the blue. Some of you believe that you create your own reality but that others do not create theirs—especially little babies who have all kinds of things happen to them or children who are abused. It is a difficult concept for many of you to grasp that seemingly helpless children or starving people also create their own reality. Whenever you buy into the victim mentality, you send people the idea that they are powerless and you make that probability one for yourselves. You must learn to honor other people's dramas and lessons. Realize that the newspaper is not going to tell you about the potential for change that exists for all of those involved in a particular scenario, because newspapers do not report and cover things in that way. You do not understand the underlying synchronicities of events: your media exposes only the external so-called facts and ignores the rich riverbed of emotional significance that accompanies human dramas and lessons.

Those who are involved in dramas in which it looks like someone is a victim are usually so out of touch with their feelings that they do not connect how they feel with what they are thinking. Victims find victims. Victors find victors. So, please, with any newspaper event or world drama in which it looks as if people are hopeless victims, honor them and honor yourself by saluting that they created their own reality. It may not be a reality that you need to learn from—or anything you feel a need to participate in. You must understand that others must go through the realms of density to bring them to light. Sometimes the greatest enlightenment lies in the greatest catastrophes and the greatest difficulties.

When you go to a restaurant and order something you want, the chef prepares it and the waiters bring it to you. You order it; however, you don't make it. Somehow the cooks or the spiritual energy make it, yet, you select it to be put before you. It will not be put before you unless you go into the restaurant to order it in the first place. So you are responsible for it and you pay for it.

Life is the same way; life is like a restaurant. Learn how to order what you want from life like you do in a restaurant and then trust that, because you ordered it, it will be put before you. When you go into a restaurant, you don't worry over every item and wonder whether or not you deserve to have it. Well, sometimes you do. Sometimes you say, "Well, I don't deserve to have that. That costs fifteen dollars. I can only have something that costs seven dollars or less."

The way you act in restaurants is a wonderful indication of the way you act in life. It is an incredible teaching to understand. When you go into a restaurant, do you simply order and say, "This is what I want," and trust that it is going to come to you, or do you worry that they are going to screw it up? As soon as the order is in, do you follow the waiter into the kitchen and say, "Oh, they probably won't have the right lettuce. They probably won't sauté those onions just so, and they won't have those kind of mushrooms I want." No. You trust it will be presented to you exactly the way you want it and you let it go. When it is presented to you, you say, "Thank you." If it is not quite right, you ask for what is needed and then you proceed.

Look at the divine nonchalance you have when you order things in a restaurant. That is how you order up life. Get clear on what you want, order it and be done with it. Don't keep calling up Spirit to see if they got the order or give advice on how to fill it. You ordered it. Trust that it will come.

You are a result of your thoughts. If there is nothing else you learn on this planet, you will learn that this is the rule in this reality and the rule of many other realities. *Thought creates experience.* Why not give yourself a gift and begin to think of yourself in a capacity that is exceptional, magnificent, and uplifting; free yourselves from the need to have the rest of society agree with you. *Validate yourselves.* For some of you, this is very difficult. How do you validate yourself when you are in the habit of not doing it?

Your words are either empowering or disempowering. We want you to have the courage to live your light, so we want to emphasize to you and convince you in whatever way possible that your thoughts formulate your world. Eliminate the words *should* and *trying* from your vocabulary. If you were to pay money every time you say these words, you would be in great debt. You are in a great debt of disempowerment or impotence. *Should* implies that you are operating under someone else's sovereignty. We would like to remind you that you are sovereign unto yourself.

If someone is *trying* to put out a newsletter or *trying* to change their patterns, they can try for the rest of their life. *Trying* is not *doing*. Whenever you use the word *trying*, you will not accomplish anything because trying is an excuse: "I tried to do it. I tried. I tried." In your own life, use the words "I am creating," "I am doing," "I am manifesting," "I am intending," and "I am bringing about." Forget "I am trying."

When you become a *doer* and are able to manifest what you want in life, you set yourself up as a mirror for many people. There has been a belief that there is a limited amount of everything and that only one person or the other can be a doer or manifester. When you begin to show that you can bend the laws of reality, other people do not like it sometimes, because they think you have something they want and they can't get it unless you don't have it.

If you put yourself behind others and are afraid of having what others do not have because you think there is not enough, you do not understand that as you allow the divine principles to work in your body and anchor themselves upon the planet that you become a living example of light. You allow the underlying purpose of light to move through your vehicle and you become a living example of what others can do. This is the high vibration that we intend to teach all of you. We want you to understand that *there is no limitation.*

There is no limitation on the entire planet. Each person on the whole planet can operate in cooperation and in a uniqueness of being. Whatever gifts of spirit and materiality come your way, don't think that you are more lucky than others. Instead, simply understand that you are able to get the divine principles to work in your physical body and that you can show others how. You can say, "Listen, it works. I have been able to do it. You can do it as well."

We spend hours teaching people about not being afraid to manifest. Each of you is frightened because you grew up with an ethic that says, "Only if you work for something is it of any value. If you do not put in hard work, you cannot get things." It is imperative for all of you to look at this idea of hard work and where it came from. Look at your parents and the belief systems they have had. We are talking about birthing a consciousness that represents the new human species that learns how to do things *effortlessly.*

If something is not being done effortlessly, then forget it. If it looks like it is too much work, something is telling you it is not the way. Only when something comes together effortlessly and simply fits, with no one doing too much to it, is it right. If you all begin to live like this, you will completely change how the species of consciousness approaches life. It is not irresponsible or a cop-out—it is a new way of carrying bricks from one place to another.

One time we talked about a big pile of bricks with a group of people and asked them, "How do you move the bricks?" They all said, "Well, you pick them up one by one." And we said, "No one ever thought of hiring someone else to do it?"

If your assignment is moving bricks from here to there, how are you going to do it? Your first answer may be, "Well, I will move them. I'll pick them up." However, you could go call someone up and say, "Move these bricks for me." If you do that, you are still doing the assignment. You are doing what needs to be done. Do you think we are going to chastise you if you don't do it yourself? No. You are still getting the job done. You see the difference?

Money seems to be an issue with everyone. You all have very definitive beliefs about how money comes to you. The more you believe you must work hard for money, the harder you are going to have to work. Many of you believe it is quite normal to work hard for money, and that if you don't work hard for money then it is "dirty." Let us ask you to remember the word *effortless* and incorporate it into your vocabulary. Say to yourself, "I am effortlessly intending that this come about." To be effortless is to command to reality to bring itself to you in a way that gives room for plenty of energy to be expended in other experimentation.

Remember, your reality is a result of your thoughts. If you believe that things are hard, what are you creating? Many of you have spent lifetimes honoring and respecting family members or people of society whom you believe are uplifting citizens and who represent to you a certain work ethic and value system. You have not thought to question this work ethic or to see if there is any other way. So you believe that in order to get money you must expend a great amount of energy, or you must be employed by someone who is going to give it to you, or whatever. These ideas are completely and totally erroneous. We cannot emphasize that enough. When you are allowing, Spirit will compensate you in a variety of unexpected ways. The only reason this has not happened before is that you just haven't believed it was possible. When you believe things are possible, reality changes.

State of mind is the name of the game here. We cannot emphasize that to you enough: how you feel about reality and how you program reality is how you are going to respond to it or how it is going to present itself to you. That is why we say, "Go for it! Be outrageous! Do what excites you! Do the impossible!" You can do it. You can do whatever you want to do. You will transform your world no matter what state the world is in.

Remember, when you learn the rules of the game—that you are a result of thought, and that this is a law within your universe—all you need do is think of how you want to be, and so you shall be. Once you figure this out, you can design your body, you can design your age, and you can fix everything about yourself, because you will be self-motivated, self-empowered, and self-generated.

TWELVE

It's an Awesome Task to Carry Light

It is time for all of you to redefine your own identities in a much greater sense. Events are transpiring in the cosmos that you and even many of your political leaders have no idea of. You must stop this foolishness about your definitions of gods—thinking that there are beings who come from the skies to this planet with special talents and abilities and that they are all spiritually connected. You are going to discover as a species some very disturbing ideas over the next number of years. We are preparing you by decree of the Family of Light so that you can understand and be informed about your own options.

We have stressed with you this idea of multidimensionality—the concept that you can be in many places and can shift your consciousness. We have shared with you the idea that there will be a number of worlds created out of this Earth. At one time or another, you will come to doubt everything we have shared with you. Your system will be shocked, and you will not want to believe the extent to which you have been uninformed, so you will deny the validity of our information for a time.

We can only offer you information based upon your own acceleration. You must evolve yourselves and have your wits about you to *ask* for information because there is a divine law concerning interference. There are many who have broken that law and interfered with Earth: even those in our own ancestral realm have done so. We have said to you often enough that this is a free-will universe and a free-will zone so that, of course, the underlying theme is that all is allowed. Therefore, there are always those who wish to be the lords and masters and authorities over others. You have been too simplistic about how many beings control others here.

The Family of Light has been noted for its penchant or predilection for creating societies in which there is a tremendous movement in all directions along the light rays. What does this mean? Light is information, so the Family of Light is the family of information. There are consciousnesses—families of war—that spend perhaps billions of years in your conception of time studying, promoting, and experiencing control over consciousness. In a universe that exists outside of the limitation of time, all scenarios within a free-will zone get played out.

This is a time for you to radically change your views about yourselves and to break down boundaries. It is time for you to rise out of the pettiness of day-to-day dramas and events and begin to connect on a cosmic level with the higher drama that is occurring. In this way, you can be better informed about your own intentions, purposes, and drama. You must be able to understand both your identity and your ability to ride your identity into any world you choose.

This story of the Family of Light, or "The Return of the White T-Shirts," as we like to call it, is *who you are*. You have committed to do a certain task, to be on assignment, and to remember and fulfill what you came here to do. We have told you that your worlds and your identity within them are going to change drastically, and you are coming closer to those times. You have had changes, many of you. If you look back to see who you were one year ago, ideally each of you will see that you are now much more empowered.

Ideally, each of you is beginning to feel that you do, in every instant, create your own reality, and that every situation you experience, whether you are employed or unemployed, is by your own design. At this time, ideally each and every one of you has the art of manifestation down, because it is now time for you to pull the cosmic gridwork of information into your body and plug it into your psyche so that you can become a broadcaster of this data upon the planet. This is the gridwork that is fired by the light-encoded filaments outside of your body.

You must become much more discerning about what and who is coming from the skies, because you are going to be duped and tricked and you are not going to understand it. We see this because we ourselves know how easy it is to dupe and trick you. Sometimes we do it to you to move you along. We told you that we have already been very tricky with you. This was necessary, because if we told you the whole story, many of you would have turned tail and run a long time ago.

Ideally, we have instilled confidence in you. We have also instilled in you a new codicil of information so that you can take the basic building block of this system—the concept that you *create yourselves*, that *you create your reality by your thoughts*—and formulate a world designed by the Family of Light. In this way, a plan and new gridwork can overlay a portion of this Earth so that a completely new probability can burst forward. Without you and the new probability that you are bringing, there is potential for a great cosmic war here upon Earth at some time.

Reach out with your feeling center and feel the confusion that is spreading around this world about what is going on. This planet has operated on a very low frequency, a frequency based on survival, and a frequency based on disempowerment. Your identity has been based on what you could gather outside of yourself. The twelve helixes will render irrelevant everything that has represented and surrounded the two helixes. All of the money saved and property owned—all of the security based on the first two helixes that provides you with identity—is completely irrelevant to the evolution of the planet.

Feel the fear and uncertainty running through the lives of humans as they begin to realize that the way their lives have been defined is now crumbling. Realize that light is the culprit of this crumbling and that you, as members of the Family of

Light and Keepers of Frequency, are causing this crumbling to take place because you carry the electromagnetic charge onto the planet that broadcasts the new frequency. You help create this chaos of new consciousness.

Think back over your own lives for the last year or two and realize that there have been times when you, yourselves, have been in an incredible chaos of consciousness. You have been in a chaos of decisions about who you are, where you want to live, who you want to mate with, whether you want to stay mated or not, whether you want to have a child or not, whether you want to continue to be a parent, and many other things.

Reach your minds out into your communities and feel how the foundation that people have based their lives on is slowly slipping away to rubble. The global grasp of reality is going, going, gone. The foundation is sliding away, and there are those who cannot see the slide at this time. The most significant reason for this slide is that there is new information accessible that makes the old information archaic and decrepit, and you are responsible for this. So you are responsible to a certain extent for evolving yourselves through this and for being your own forms of inspiration—for being living examples for others.

You take a very active role. There are many who say, "Oh, no, here comes the light!" because light is known to alter every vibrational frequency that it encounters. Light carries information, and information expands systems so that old systems can no longer exist. So, as light moves to destroy, it also births new systems by what it leaves behind. A new order is formed.

Some of you find it difficult to think of yourselves as destroyers because you have a belief system about destruction. It is a paradigm, and if you get stuck in that vibration and do not smash those ideas, you will become very confined and restricted in experiencing reality. Yes, you are definitely destroyers. You destroy systems where the dark team and ignorance prevail. Light goes in to destroy all systems, and the experience of destruction is relative to how strong or with what fervor consciousness clings to what is being destroyed.

Who's going to bail you out when the going gets rough? Where is the rescue team? *You are it.* In order to have this transformation take place, you must use what you have to bring it about. There is incredible assistance from all kinds of realms; however, it all depends on you, not us. You are going to change the frequency simply by commitment, determination, and willpower.

Discover what you are in your physical body because it is your outreach of power here. Learn to direct and use it and become one with it. By carrying light inside of your body, you bring that frequency onto the planet, and that frequency has information. The frequency of light contains the history of your identity and the history of your particular consciousness. As we have said, that consciousness was scattered from your database or cellular structure because those who came in to be your gods could not control you if you had the same abilities they did. So they did the biogenetic experimentation and mutation that has been called "the Fall." That was when the ignorance of the human species became more predominant. They performed many different experimentations, which went on for a very long period of time.

Light represents the putting together of what has been asunder, and to perform that task all you have to do is *be.* As you simply *are,* and as you evolve yourself and let your own personal life evolve, *truly* you are to take for granted that all the other members of light are evolving as you are. You send your telepathic broadcast out that your presence is here, much as we always say to you, "We are here." We are also members of the Family of Light, and we bring information with us and broadcast it everywhere.

There is a need for each of you to examine the boundaries you have set around yourself. You believe that you have evolved, that you have a large picture, and that you see many things. And, relative to where you have journeyed from, indeed you have made progress. However, we guarantee you that you are not seeing the boundaries that you presently set for yourself, which still define what you believe you can and cannot do. They are what tethers you to this version or frequency of reality.

These boundaries that you set, and that you advertise and announce about yourselves, keep you from moving with the information that is awakening inside you. The information is part of the spiritual upliftment. Different layers of reality are removed so that you become more in tune with the realms of spirit. That is what spiritual advancement is. We want you to give up boundaries and stop defining and protecting every aspect of your lives.

It is an awesome task to carry light. Once you allow light to come into your body, you begin the process of change—which is not always joyous, uplifting, and fun filled, as some of you have discovered. In this process, when things are not so fun filled, the first thing you may do to keep yourself from evolving and changing is to respond to emotional events with fear. You may blame someone else and whine and complain, and you may feel and believe that someone did something to you.

The rest of the planet believes this, but they are not members of the Family of Light. There are millions of members of the Family of Light here, of course, and light is returning to this planet where the Dark T-Shirts were in charge for a very long time. The Dark T-Shirts have fed off your emotions of fear and negativity and war and greed; because this is a free-will universe, all of this has been allowed. Prime Creator is the dark team as well as the Family of Light. Prime Creator is *all* things.

We teach you in stories. Someday, perhaps, you will see through the stories we tell. You will not need them any longer, and you will be able to smash paradigms and come into a knowing of larger realities. Until that day, we speak to you in stories so that we can hold your interest and entice you into areas you are petrified to go—areas where you have committed in the deepest portion of your soul to journey.

In a short period of time there will be a great need to realize which people are really Keepers of Frequency and which are just talking about it. The Keepers of Frequency are going to be called upon to create a certain stability upon this planet, for they know 100 percent of the time that they create their reality. They learn how to defy the laws of humanity by conscious direction of their awareness and energy. That is the depth of impeccability and commitment we are speaking of.

We are not here to bandy words or get you to feel good about yourself. We are here to remind you who you are and what you have agreed to do—what you have come here to achieve on this planet. We are here to be your cheerleaders and encourage you to remember—to give some guidance and assistance so that you can discover for yourselves the miracle that awaits inside the human body.

The way you can best operate at this time is to be keepers of your own frequency and not go around "saving" everyone else. Do everything in your power to keep yourself consistently aware and understanding of what is going on. Be consistent with the frequency of light that brings you information, and with the frequency of love, which is the frequency of creation.

As the food source is taken away from the creator gods and the frequency barrier is pierced, Earth's gridwork will change. In actuality, Earth is going through an initiation. Earth cares about all of its inhabitants and is evolving as its inhabitants are evolving into an existence in which greater possibilities will be everyday occurrences—in which miracles can become the way of life because they will exist within the frequency that will become available. Each of you assists in making that frequency alive on this planet by living your life according to light and according to what you know. This is work of an individual nature. You may work in groups and have certain leaders, but you must, as individuals, evolve yourselves. As you do so, and as you are led by your light to live a certain way, you will begin to feel excited.

You do not have to work with us or with *anyone* continuously to gather information. The only continuity needed is for you to continuously work with yourself and seek the meaning of what we call the exalted self. Feel what *the exalted self* means— it is triumphant, liberated, joyous in achievement, and the highest in attainment.

This planet is in desperate need of committed entities who are in search of the exalted self. The continuity we have been speaking of—that it will behoove you to bring into your lives— involves knowing from moment to moment inside your beings that you are committed to discovering this exaltation. This exaltation can be translated in words as a frequency, or wave of feeling, or vibration. You all understand vibration in terms of light and sound. Vibrations are ongoing—they carry and transmit forms of intelligence. When you look to yourself and do not forget that you are on this path—and you continuously remind yourself that you are pulling light into your body and are seeking to raise the frequency of your physical being, defy the laws of humanity, and alter the frequency of the planet—you are producing a kind of continuity that can do more than all the books and tapes in the world.

There is nothing stronger than your commitment to the exalted self. Once you commit yourself to the energy of light, the energy of exaltation, and uplifted frequency, you are marked. Then you must live according to what these energies put before you as you call for your task to be accelerated.

First and foremost, *live your light*. Live that light inside of yourself with courage. Don't live in the closet—*live it*. Speak what you know without getting up on a soap box and waving your hands around like a fanatic. Simply state, "This is what I believe. This is what I live." For example, someone may say to you, "Careful, you might catch a cold." You can say in return, "I don't believe in catching colds. I don't use my body for sickness." By saying things like this, you bring others to awakening. Speak what you know in casual conversation with family and friends.

Wherever you are, use the pillar of light. We recommend that each of you visualize a pillar of light coming in through the top of your head, opening your crown, and filling your body with light. Picture this cosmic pillar of light coming from the higher cosmos, filling you, and then coming out your solar plexus and making a ball of light around your body so that you exist within a glowing etheric egg.

When you love yourself and Earth, and you know that you are here to redefine, redesign, and break the boundaries of humanity, you broadcast this. You live your life committed to this. If you ask us how much time you need to devote to this, we will say, "It is very simple: *all of your time.*" All of it. It is not something you worry about, it is something you simply *are.* You live it—it is your divinity. You will find that when you live your light, you will draw to yourself others who are very interested in living their lives in the same manner, and your numbers will grow and grow.

When you make the commitment to say, "Spirit, I am wishing to be employed by you. Put me to work and show me what I can do. Give me the opportunity to live my light, to speak my truth, and to carry this light around the globe," then Spirit will put you to work. Be clear on what you are available for and make a contract with Spirit. Tell Spirit what you want for compensation. Spirit will allow you to negotiate and write whatever contract you want as long as you are operating in a capacity of service to yourself to uplift your vibration. When you are in service to yourself and are committed to personally evolving and changing, you uplift everyone around you. That is service. Service is not going out and martyring yourself and saying, "I'm going to save you." Service is doing the work yourself and living in such a way that everyone you touch is affected by your journey.

There is nothing wrong with getting a little feisty with Spirit and saying, "Listen guys, I've had it. I've been asking and I'm willing to do it. Please, I want acceleration." If you want an acceleration, be clear, be very prepared to take off, and be open to reading the symbols as they come to you. When a book falls off a shelf, read it. When an opportunity comes for you to go somewhere, don't say, "I'm sorry—I can't afford it." *Do it.* When a person is put in your path, and you have been saying you want a relationship, but the person has the wrong packaging, *do it.* You are operating in no sense, and perhaps these things are Spirit's way of bringing you pattern breakers. If you are clear and you communicate in every situation, you can make a lot of progress.

You all think too much about how things are going to come about and what the packaging is going to look like. This is important to realize. So when you ask for an acceleration, be prepared to take chances that the logical mind may scream about. The logical mind is going to kick and fuss over some of these things because it will be afraid. As soon as you hear yourself say "I can't do that" or "That doesn't make any sense," listen. These are key words. Simply say, "I am divinely guided. I am intending an acceleration. I am intending that I work through an uplifting capacity, and I will take a chance on this. This feels right even though it makes no sense, so I will go for it." However, if it doesn't *feel good* and it doesn't make any sense, then don't do it. Trust your feelings.

There is a culling going on—a culling of the chosen. What does it mean to be called "the chosen?" Those who gather when we speak and those who hear the sound of their internal song are the chosen. Just because you are the chosen does not mean you are automatically going to rise in the ranks and perform the duty that needs to be performed. Who chose you? *You chose yourselves.* You are not members of an exclusive club—and yet, on the other hand, you are. The membership in this club is voluntary, and all of you decided who you would be and why you would come here. We cannot emphasize enough that courage is going to become the middle name for each and every one of you.

Many of you have lives that are in the closet. You are not willing to let everyone know what your intimate beliefs are. You may feel very safe in a room discussing a variety of subjects, some of them very far out, yet, in your workplace or with your family or whatever, you put a zipper across your mouth and will not give yourself permission to speak your truth.

There are a multitude of people whose codings are waiting to hear your voice. So you, the chosen, are being culled at this time. You are being sorted out for courage. If you cannot gather courage now, we are not too certain that you are going to gather courage later on.

You each came to this planet to do a task, and that task is at hand. *It is now.* The decade of change is upon you, and as you integrate and realize what this change means, it will alter each and every one of your lives. The change means giving up many things, coming apart from many things, and coming together with other things because you will trust. *Trust* is the word that all of you would love to have as your middle name, and yet trust is something you all say that you don't have.

What does it mean to trust? It means to have such inner knowing that your thoughts create your world—to simply be quite certain, with divine nonchalance and inner knowing, that *if you think something, it is.* It is this theme over and over again that we are attempting to present to you, in every capacity and every means of expression, so that one of these days you will get it. Once you get it and begin to live it, you will begin to change your lives.

We keep emphasizing that the time to get moving is now. It is not necessarily that you have run out of time. It is that time is beginning to squeeze itself in upon you, and if you do not act, things can move into discomfort. As we said, there is a culling of the chosen. You have chosen yourselves; therefore, if you do not move into the work of the blueprint you have designed for yourselves, to a certain extent you will run out of time. You have a few more years before things will be so topsy-turvy and hectic that if you are not living your life in the true eminence of light ave volunteered to, it could be too late. In other words, if you procrastinate and procrastinate, you will be washed into the undertow of the tidal wave as it comes—perhaps literally.

No matter what the endeavor in which you are being led to participate, it is part of your blueprint and plan so that you can evolve. And by evolving, you affect the evolution of the planet. Everything you do is for your evolution. As you come into comprehension of who humans are and what this place is, you begin to open new pathways for others. You will find that events you never imagined will somehow be put together before you. These will be things that are beyond your comprehension— "setups," as we like to call them, or opportunities you never thought of. This is when you will know that you are living your light and doing so with courage.

There is a good possibility that light carriers will come into question in the next few years. Understand that this is part of the plan. All of you must have a clear intention as to how you would like your reality to be designed. This does not mean that you are not flexible; it means that you operate with clarity. You say, "To my guides and all of those who are assisting me in my evolutionary journey on Earth: It is my intention that I be successful. It is my intention that I be always safe in all things that I do. It is my intention that I receive love and give love in all things that I do. It is my intention that I have a good time and that I be provided for with prosperity according to my needs. It is my intention that I not become overly enamored of the material world."

Though you must do your own work to evolve, there are many off-planetary and nonphysical beings ready to work with you. All you need do is call them for assistance. When you do, always state clearly that any assistance come to you from light. Stay in your integrity and be aware. On this planet, it is assumed that if someone is intelligent they are spiritually aware. *This is absolutely a falsehood!* Someone can be brilliant and learn to transcend human laws and yet still not operate with the frequency of light or the frequency of love. Be aware of this and be clear about the assistance you call to yourself.

We have mentioned many times that light frequency brings information. Love frequency brings creation as well as respect for and connection to all of creation. Love frequency without light frequency can be very crippling. If you think that love frequency comes from something outside of yourself instead of from inside yourself, you will do what has been done on this planet over and over again: worship someone who is promoting love frequency as if they were a saint.

The ideal is to carry the light frequency of information—to become informed—and to couple it with love frequency. This will allow you to feel a part of creation and to not judge it or be frightened by it but simply to see the divinity and perfection of it as it evolves to teach every included consciousness about itself.

THIRTEEN

Whose Purpose Are You?

We said that you exist for a purpose. Whose purpose? Did you ever think of that one? Whose purpose are you?

You have purpose because all aspects of consciousness are connected to one another. None exist outside the system; they are all parts of the whole. That is the purpose we want you to seek. The essence of the vehicle you occupy and the energy you generate are part of a developmental sequence that you can say has a purpose for your personal search in life. But what purpose do you add to the whole? Can you conceive of someone else using your purpose and growing from it? An energy that you do not know exists?

This universe is interlocked in such a way that it is based on the domino system. All aspects of consciousness have gathered in this universe to affect each other because that is the only way consciousness in this particular system can experience itself. In another system or another universal structure, each and every type of consciousness may be completely free. In other words, you could be on your own and serve no purpose to anyone else. That is not true in this universe.

There are many different universes and themes. Just like one hundred pennies make a dollar, certain collections of universes make something that is a collection of energies. Eventually, you will begin to fathom and recognize that there are whole systems of existence that have nothing to do with existence as you are working with it. This system is designed as a free-will zone, within which everything is interlocking and interworking with everything else.

There are other kinds of zones, which perhaps you could also call free-will zones, where everything is independent of everything else. Here on Earth, everything is interlocked with everything else. There is much more space in a system in which everything is independent. Or, let us say, there is much more *awareness* of space, not necessarily space. That kind of universe could in actuality be much smaller than this universe, but because it is not operating out of density, the awareness of space could be greater.

Your purpose is to carry information and, by carrying it, to make the information accessible to others by frequency. When we share a story with you, you end up carrying information. Information is light; light is information. The more you become informed, the more you alter your frequency. You are electromagnetic creatures, and everything that you are, you broadcast to everyone else. Just as you can recognize someone in fear, you can recognize someone in joy if you begin to learn how to use your body to tune into this kind of recognition.

Your assignment is to carry information and to evolve yourself to the highest capability within the human form. When you do this, you cannot help but affect multitudes. You may feel that your particular occupation is not on a grand scale—say, for instance, you are a waitress. Remember, things are not what they appear to be on the outside, and everyone you come in contact with is affected by your vibration. Some of you may be left in very menial or mundane jobs for a while, or you may be led simply to be parents and guardians of your children, or you may do work that you feel is not exactly on the road to high glory. Yet you will have a certain time period in which you must assimilate all of this information that is indeed radical. You must fit it into your life, and you must fit it into the history of your world by living it, perceiving it, and getting used to it. Once you can consistently maintain a frequency of information and not be riding the roller coaster of emotions up and down because you don't know who you are, you will be given a task. It will be put before you, and it will be part of your blueprint. Your blueprint is your own personal detailed plan or outline of action for this lifetime. Many of you already know your blueprint and what you will be guided to. Each of you knows your plan in the deepest portion of your being. What gets in the way of your knowing is logically thinking that you don't have the talent for your plan or that you can't do it. If you go into a meditative state, you will receive a picture of your identity and reality and the next step of your assignment day by day. Meditation is a state of communication; it is not a way to go somewhere to get lost. Meditation is a way to get informed and to go to a place that nourishes you.

You will move into your purpose and, more than likely, it will have to do with facilitating the frequency: transducing it, stepping it down to others, explaining it, using it to heal others, and stabilizing it for the human race. When each of you can hold a frequency of information without freaking out and can be counted upon to be consistent, then you anchor the frequency on the planet. That frequency is recognized. It cannot be traced, exactly, but it can be recognized, and it is being recognized now. That is why there has been a frenzied step-up to alter that frequency. You will see more frequency control everywhere you look, only now you will be able to recognize it for what it is.

You will find that all the things in your life have prepared you step by step for what you will be doing. At one time, perhaps, you were a Boy Scout leader and learned how to work with young boys. Maybe at another time you worked in a restaurant and learned how to work with food and to serve. Through your jobs, you created certain aspects of reality so that later on, when you must teach these systems how to go beyond themselves, you have an idea where these humans are coming from.

We speak to you as if you are not human because, to us, you are not. To us, you are members of the Family of Light, and we know your multidimensional selves. We speak to you about dealing with humans because it is your assignment to integrate with them, soothe them, and awaken a spark of light within them so that they are not all destroyed and so that this place can house a new species and a new realm of activity.

We have talked many times about the evolving DNA and the frequency modulation that has kept the species and the experiment controllable and manageable. You have been hired and are on assignment from the future to catapult back into this cycle of existence—to incarnate many times so that you can understand what has kept humans controlled. In this way, you can operate from the inside and change the system. When you are in a battle with your logical mind, you are experiencing a conflict between the portion of yourself that is human, which has bought the story, and a portion of yourself that is Family of Light, which has not bought the story and is learning about the bigger picture.

Begin to realize that the portion of yourself that operates out of logic is teaching you something. It is giving you first-hand experience of how most of the population operates and first-hand knowledge of what you are going to have to work around to reach others. If it were quite easy for you to move into intuition and operate there completely out of trust, and if you did not have this duality of understanding with the logical mind, in the long run you would become very impatient with the rest of humanity. If it were easy for you, how could you possibly understand how difficult it is for others?

Humans have been controlled by frequency for a long time. They are so used to this frequency control and the logical mind has been so overly developed in recent times that there is much suspicion and fear—a dark place of self that is so controlled that people are frightened to even go into it and trust that they could possibly receive information on their own. When you think of the entities who have modulated the way humans broadcast themselves by rearranging their DNA and instituting various scenarios and events upon this planet—and then funneling the results of this psychic energy through different portals out into space for their own reasons—you can see what you are battling.

There are those who want you and the whole planet to function in no other way but through logic—a very fearful logic. The best advice we can offer you at this time is to use that logic. Say, "I will be in logic here for a moment and see what my logical mind is doing. It is wanting to take over. It has been told that this is how it is. I have also been told that this other stuff is true too. I will simply observe how I waiver between one and the other. Am I angry? Am I insecure? What brings me upliftment? What brings me security? What does each mode of thinking do for me? What am I perceiving about myself? How am I feeling?"

Observe and acknowledge all of this. Then say, "Now that I've given everyone a chance to be on stage, what do *I* want?" Reaffirm what *you* want, and you know you want to evolve. Do you see how cycling back through doubt is in actuality part of the Divine Plan? It is part of understanding what others who will be following in your footsteps will go through. You must learn to open your compassion center or heart center, which is probably one of the most difficult things to do. Learn to feel compassion for yourself and for everyone else, as you all have the courage to let go and feel.

It is very important to observe how you deal with events. Different events are brought to you so that you can observe them. Learn to observe your behavior and to spend much more time alone—even if sometimes it is difficult for you and you feel lonely. In the long run, you will thank us for directing you to have a more meaningful encounter with yourself. You hold the richness and ripeness that can bring you into higher realization.

There is an order that you operate within that part of yourself cannot see. Sometimes when part of yourself is operating without vision or seeing, events occur to get you back on track. Be aware that, in this new chaos of consciousness and confusion and shifting of uncertainty, there is a divine order.

This could be compared to baking a cake. Each ingredient in the recipe is of itself an integral whole and has its own sense of structure: the eggs, the flour, the butter, the sugar. When you begin to put them all together, it looks as if you are making chaos. Someone could say, "You are wrecking everything. You wrecked that egg. Where did the sugar go? You are wrecking all of the essential elements here." They don't understand, perhaps, the magic of the catalytic formula of heat.

There is a catalytic energy present at this time on the planet as all of the individual structures begin to melt and merge to create what looks like chaos. There will be something new born out of this, just like a cake is born out of the chaos of mixing together certain ingredients. Someone who does not understand that after you mix cake batter, you put it in the oven to bake it, could look at the goopy batter and think they made nothing. Many people on the planet will not recognize that there is a higher order behind the chaos—that there is a recipe being followed.

Each of you has a specific assignment within this recipe. Of course, you have free will to determine how you will follow the recipe and be an ingredient of it. This free will allows you to decide the specifics of how you would like your life to be designed, although you must live out your blueprint. Whether you choose to do this with difficulty or with ease, in poverty or in richness, is up to you. It all depends on where you have been convinced to put your boundaries.

What can we say to convince you to take all of your boundaries down—to stop limiting what you believe can be yours? If there is anything we wish to achieve, it is to have each of you boundless and free, knowing that every thought you entertain somehow determines your experience. If we could get you to live 100 percent of the time according to what you want, we would feel that this has been a most successful year.

We are going to ask each of you to make that commitment and to live a cleaner and more impeccable life. We ask you to accept responsibility in areas that you have not even thought of accepting responsibility. We want you each to act as if you know what is going on. Act as if you are divinely guided in every choice you make, and begin to believe that you are always at tne right place at the right time. Say to yourself, "I am in divine guidance. I am always at the right place at the right time. Everything I do is orchestrated for my higher growth, my higher consciousness, and my higher evolution." We want you to operate in that way all of the time now. Be living Keepers of Frequency. When light is brought into your body, it fires your light-encoded filaments and helps rebundle the DNA, creating a frequency change. Frequency is what you know. *Frequency is your identity.*

There have been periods when many different dimensions have existed upon this planet at the same time. In the last thousand years, there has been a receding of the many different dimensions as great chaos and darkness have come over the population. These dimensions or other realities or places where the laws of existence are a bit different are returning. You help them return by pulling the dimensions onto this planet and creating what is called a dimensional merge.

Sometimes you move into these dimensions and do not recognize that you are in them. You enter an altered state, part-icularly when you go to a sacred site on Earth. You move in-to a different dimensional frequency and everything changes. You feel uplifted and full of energy, or sick to your stomach. Something goes on when you move into an altered state.

Since you are in the altered state, you do not always *know* you are in it. That is the beginning of the dimensional merge. When you return home from a sacred site, you may look back and say, "Wow, what happened there?" That is the feeling of ex-periencing different dimensions.

Dimensional *collisions* are another story. Those who are gripped with fear and refuse to change, even though their pur-pose is to be on the planet at this time to change, will experience the dimensions as collisions. The dimensional merge for them will be like a solid wall of cement hitting another solid wall of cement. Great discomfort will occur on this planet for many. This is already occurring on a very small scale as discomfort in the nervous system. People may develop disease of the nervous system simply because of their refusal to evolve and change their stand about themselves and their reality. All of you who are working with other humans, whether you are medical people, bodyworkers, teachers, musicians, or whatever, understand that this is the human dilemma: *the need to shift the definition of self and reality.*

Use your will and mind to decide how you would like reality to construct itself. By doing this, you will eventually discover that there is a higher will and a higher plan, and you will ride your consciousness to it and discover the divine path. This divine path has in mind the evolution of consciousness. You, as a human species, have believed for eons what others have told you about yourselves. As we have said, there has been a purpose to this: others have wanted to control you. Strive as you would for attainment, it was difficult on the planet because the DNA was scattered and closed down, so no matter what you wanted, the vibrational connections were not available. Now that the vibrational connections are coming onto the planet, the Divine Plan—which you can think of as a grid or blueprint—is coming closer to Earth, and the dimensions are going to meet eventually. When they are going to meet is up to you. The Divine Plan is not scheduled to come here on a specific date; it depends on how quickly humans can meet the needs and master themselves.

What does it mean to master yourself? In order to understand the Divine Plan and move into the blueprint, you must look at yourself. You must be able to master *who you are*. There are many things in your society for which you must master a test in order to say, "Yes, I qualify. I have mastered these rules, and I utilize them and put them to my will." For example, you must master how to drive a car to get a license. How many of you can master your bodies and use them with your will? Very few.

Why? Because no one told you it was possible. We are here to remind you of a number of things.

Earth at this time is a very difficult place to be, simply because those who are coded to bring the changes onto the planet are coded to teach themselves. You see, the problem on this planet, over and over again, has been the gods. One god after another. Who have the gods been? The gods created you. You are their project. You are dear to them. However, some of them you are not very dear to because they do not understand emotion and feelings. And some of them are enamored of different realities than you are.

Consciousness is allowed its expression, and you have been allowed your expression within limitation by those who have been governing you. From your point of view, you have never let them govern you and you have no idea that they exist. They bring dramas onto this planet in the guise of what you call religion, leadership, or, sometimes, inspiration. Events, even though they are orchestrated to achieve certain things, sometimes gather those who hang on, and many other probabilities come out other than what was intended.

We want to communicate to you that there is a drastic change going on. We cannot emphasize this enough. Earth is in for a big shake-up. The shake-up involves humanity processing and conceiving of data that is totally out of the current paradigm. This means that your nervous system will be assaulted with data and must be able to unlock itself from how it believes it controls or perceives reality.

The task for you members of the Family of Light who have desired to take this information inside of yourselves is to anchor a new frequency on the planet by anchoring it impeccably inside yourselves. This is not easy. *It was not meant to be easy.* You did not come here to have an easy assignment. You are renegades, and you have *been* renegades. If we could give each of you a minute's worth of your multidimensional memories, you would know what we are talking about. You would know in the deepest portion of your being that time and time again, in different guises and different collections of form, you have gone where change needed to be anchored. You have gone many times, busted the paradigms, liberated yourselves, and moved beyond where you thought your identity was. This is the Divine Plan: merging the self.

The Divine Plan has many ramifications and brings together many kinds of forces. You have heard us talk about the forces of light and the forces of darkness. We have nicknamed them the "White T-Shirts" and the "Dark T-Shirts" to make the situation neutral and have you know it is a game. We also want you to know that there is a grave seriousness to the game and that in and around and above the game is the Divine Plan. The Divine Plan can be anchored as a vibration into certain human bodies that are coded for this and that came here to carry this frequency. Then you can rise to your own blueprint of impeccability.

When your own life rises to a position where you do not even recognize it as your life, you allow the energy of the non-physical realms to use you as a conduit—to merge the dimensions and liberate consciousness into a new way of perceiving. Even though there is death and destruction coming to your world, remember that death and destruction come in the autumn every year on this planet. The flowers and leaves on the trees are killed by the frost; things wither and die. Perhaps someone who lives where it is always summer would be very disturbed when they saw autumn for the first time. They would think, "Goodness, the world is being destroyed here. All the beauty is being taken away." Understand that this is what is going on with Earth. It is a season when some things will die so that many new things can be born. It is all part of the Divine Plan.

FOURTEEN

Emotions—The Secret in the Chronicles of Time

There are those who exist in this universe who have yet to discover human emotion. When you visit Earth's ancient lands and look at the creations of other times and places, you can feel the frequencies and vibrations inherent in the sites. You *know* that there are keys there, and you *know* that there are messages— that there is something locked within that once existed and will surface again. In the same way, human beings have something hidden within them that is very valuable for the evolution of the universe. We refer to this data as the codes and master numbers: geometric formulae of light that are integral to recreating and producing life forms throughout this universe.

Human beings have been tucked away, hidden, and forgotten in the antiquities of time ever since their DNA was rearranged, because it is in the distant past of the chronicles of time when the species was alive and vibrating very differently. That time has been forgotten or shelved by some. As we have said, you have been in quarantine, almost as if you have been in the dungeons of time for so long that as the new eras have come forward they have forgotten that you have been here.

There are those, however, who have not forgotten. They have sent you on assignment to change all of this: to bring memory forward and *to bring the value of human existence back to the forefront of creation.* You are needed because you carry something that many other species have no idea of: emotion. And just as you need to work together to bring your own selves into a wholeness and richness of multidimensional being, there are those who are striving to catapult the entire universe into a new octave—a reach toward and creation of new territory.

The Keepers of Time know where the data is locked, and you have been found; you have been selected to bring it into the light. We have come forward—or backward from our time period—to assist those of you on assignment to unlock the annals of human DNA. We are here to help you rearrange them within your own being and then to become part of the Living Library.

As we have mentioned, what is occurring on Earth is going to affect things in many places. Energy is being sent here at this time to redirect certain universal forces so that they will come into alignment and bring this universe into simultaneous awareness of its identity. What is in Earth is like a locked-away secret in the chronicles of time, and it has to do with emotion. In this gift of emotion there is wealth and richness; there is incredible ability to transcend many different realities and to move through and experience many different states of awareness. Emotion allows certain energies to coalesce, fuse, bond, and come together in realization of themselves. Without emotion, that bond could not be.

There are those existing in this universe who are very ancient and who have come to the realization of what this place is. They have been working for eons. They are ancient elders even to our system, and they are honored as great wise men and women, in your terms, although they are not men or women at all. They are thought of as the Keepers of Existence in this system. They are the ones who make the movements and drive the system like a pilot drives a ship. They steer this universe on its course; that is their job. Just like you have jobs, their job is to steer this universe on a course of discovery. They have discovered from their own learning and journey that they must connect with other universes.

There is a plan to catapult and send energy into new experience. At this time, Earth and a number of other systems where you simultaneously exist are instrumental in the reemergence of emotion, with the purpose of comprehending all identities compacted into one. The universes are discovering what they can do by coming together and interworking just as you are discovering what you can become. There is no preconceived idea of what will happen. *This is new territory.*

Emotion is the key to all of this. As human beings, you need emotion to connect you with your spiritual self. Emotion is essential to understanding spirituality because *emotion generates feeling.* The mental body and physical body are very linked, as are the emotional body and spiritual body. The spiritual body is, of course, the body that exists beyond physical limitation. You need emotions to comprehend the nonphysical, which is why emotions have been so controlled upon this planet. You have been allowed very little room emotionally and have been encouraged to feel powerless or frightened.

Many of you don't want to go beyond these emotional barriers and through your personal boundaries because it might be painful. You'd like to say "abracadabra" and just have them be gone. Pain brings you feeling. If you can feel in no other way, sometimes, in order to capture your attention as a stubborn human, you create pain to show yourself the range of your abilities and to bring yourself into life. In this way, you can feel the richness of being alive.

Most human beings are afraid of their emotional or feeling center; they are afraid to feel. *Trust your feelings no matter what they are.* Trust that they lead you to something and that the way you feel can bring you a realization. You all want to be in life and be removed from it at the same time. You say, "Let me just be here and be a powerful person, but I don't want to feel or participate too much because it hurts too much and then I will get sucked down. I don't trust life."

When you are not afraid of feeling, and you move past judgment and allow yourself to feel all the ways you feel, you will have a tremendous breakthrough because you will be able to *ride feeling into other realities*. Some of you are afraid to feel and participate in this reality, let alone ride into other realities, because you do not trust your feelings. If you wish to have an acceleration, dive into something that brings up feeling. Stop skirting the issue so that you can think you are in control. Dive in the middle of it and then see if you are in control.

It's not that you don't know how to feel, it's that you are *afraid of your feelings*. You don't know what to do with them when you have them. They bring up a sense of powerlessness within you, so you associate feeling with a sense of, "Oh, no, I blew it." You have a boundary in your belief system that states that when something comes up that is emotional and brings pain or anger, then it is not good. It is time to stop tiptoeing around things and avoiding your emotions.

Anger serves a purpose. All of you want to get finished with it: you want to sweep it under the rug and act as if it is no good. You act like it is rotten vegetables, throw it out, and bury it in the back garden as if there is no purpose to it. We are emphasizing that there is a purpose to fear and a purpose to anger. If you would allow yourselves to express and experience your fears, which might lead to the expression of your anger, you would learn something. Those of you who want desperately to avoid fear and anger, and who are really afraid of these feelings, have something great to learn through these emotions. They are techniques that move you beyond your personal boundaries of identity and behavior, and you are simply afraid to experience this.

Most of the time, all you want is to be accepted. You feel that no one will like you if you do certain things or feel certain ways, so you don't give yourself permission to have those certain feelings. That is where the anger comes from. You have anger because you make judgments about what you can and cannot do. If you do not give yourself permission to feel, you cannot learn. Feeling connects you with life.

Feelings serve a variety of purposes in human beings. We encourage all of you to please trust and cultivate and rely on your feelings. Understand that your feelings are your ticket to ride into multidimensional realities, where you must go if you are seriously playing this game. In multidimensional realities, you learn to hold and focus many different versions of yourself at once. Feelings can take you to these places, particularly feelings that you trust. Many of you are very suspicious and masterful over your feelings. You will not allow certain feelings to come forward, or you judge them when they come up instead of observing where they take you or what they do for you.

Because you have a fear of something, you keep yourself from experiencing it because you put up a wall that says, "If I go there, it is bad." You put the brakes on. In actuality, your fear will eventually energize the experience into your realm of development because all thought is drawn into form based on the emotional influence behind it. So sometimes the greatest thing to do is to simply say, "What the heck, I will go there. I surrender." Then deal with being there and don't worry about being centered while you are in your feeling center. If you intend to go into your feeling center and always be in control, you are not giving yourself the range of movement that is needed to ride the emotions that knock down boundaries and belief systems.

Anger has its purpose. Anger is not purposeless and pain is not purposeless. They all lead you to something. You can make an intention to go into your feeling center and learn how to be centered there while you explore the opportunities. If you say, "I am going to be centered there," it sounds as if you won't allow yourself any movement within it. Instead, just intend to have a centeredness. A centeredness does not mean that things don't fluctuate; it means that you allow things to fluctuate. Whether a boat is ready to tip over or is in calm water, *you allow it*. You ride it, then you get out of the event either a calm ride or a rough ride. Your emotions are not just food for others, *they are food for the self*. This is how you nourish yourself and create your identity. This is your identity as frequency through your emotions. Emotions feed you and feed your call letters into existence.

You are going to deal with each of your boundaries, simply because that is what you do not want to do. You would love to say, "Golden stardust, eliminate all that has limited me. Boom! I am free!" Ideally, it would be so simple. That is a classic example of wanting to recircuit and bypass the feeling center. You have certain emotional beliefs or feelings that assist in making these boundaries outside of yourself, so when you break a boundary, you have to deal with the emotion that put the boundary there in the first place. Through your emotional body you are connected to your spiritual body. You may want to bypass something that is difficult, yet you *have to feel your way through it.*

You want to sweep difficult things under the rug and say, "I don't want to do these," when the difficult things are your gemstones. Even if you discover you have 101,000 boundaries, do not feel frustrated. Simply say, "This is interesting." Look at the boundaries you have set up and, instead of swearing at them, simply observe them and see if you can discover how they came about. See what purpose they served—what grocery store you shopped in when you bought those items.

As soon as you acknowledge and recognize and are willing to release something, it moves. When you cling or have fear or think, "I like that boundary; that serves me very well," then you limit yourself.

You must learn to *love your emotions.* As long as you describe something as difficult, you are making it difficult. No one else is. You are resisting and judging the changes coming about. You are feeling that you do not know what is going on, and you wish to be in control. Control is something very convenient and very handy. It must be applied at the right place at the right time, like super glue. Super glue in the wrong place doesn't do much good. Did you ever super glue your hands or lips together? You must learn to exercise control in the way you use super glue. If you screw up with super glue, you get stuck and you can't do anything. Control is the same way: you get stuck with it, and it sticks you to something that you don't need to be stuck to. You must be very selective about what you decide to control or not control. The old human pattern, or the paradigm that exists, says, "You must be in control."

You, as members of the Family of Light, are having an awakening. *You need your emotions.* You must become friends with your emotions because, through feelings, you can climb the ladder to the multidimensional self and the twelve-chakra system and explore what you discover. Through feelings, you can tell if something is going on or not. The logical mind will disinvolve itself when something is going on if the body is not plugged into feeling. Feeling registers frequency change. Logical mind does not register frequency change.

You are experiencing an awakening of frequency change. You are being led to change many portions of your life and to give up many things. Don't resist the changes and feel out of control because you don't know what is coming and it appears that your emotions are getting in your way. Your emotions are simply wanting to show you something; you don't like it because you think your emotions are interfering or will embarrass you.

Get clever. Next time you come into one of these emotional situations, say to yourself immediately, "Alright, I know what is going on; I'm not getting caught in this one. I know there is something here for me to learn, and something for me to change. I believe that I am guided and that I am following a blueprint, so I will check out what is in this for me by not judging it and by going with the flow. I request that all my changes come in joy and safety and harmony. That is my decree. Everything in my evolution I am intending is covered by that: I experience joy and safety and harmony. So I will go with this energy and see what is changing for me and what I need to give up."

When your memories are not intact and you have not cultivated trust inside yourself, you shut down because you don't understand what is occurring when you are made ready for change. It is imperative for people to trust the feeling center and operate with it. When "stuff" activates your feeling center and brings you into discomfort, face the feelings that you do not like. This is your essence. These feelings are your jewels, your treasures, and your gems, from which you can learn about your identity. They are your springboard, and you are never finished with them. You cannot shove them away and say, "Yuck, I don't like the me I was then!" However, you can alter the "you" who perceived reality in that way. As you continue to become aware and gain a vast comprehension of who you are, you can look back at that entity in that place and have a whole new realization of who you were then. This process is ongoing. You will begin to see it in one another.

Honor your friends as they go *through* their "stuff"; just don't get involved in it. If it is for you, do it, but don't help others prolong their dramas. It is time to move *through* "stuff," not to stage a 365-day Broadway run with it. We suggest telling your stories once or twice or three times, and that is it. You don't need to tell everyone everything, because everyone else has their "stuff" occurring too. Do you understand? When you continually speak about your "stuff," you are missing the point because you are *talking* instead of *doing* and *seeing* what you are telling yourself. By talking to everyone about what is going on with you, you are simply wanting to get attention, and you don't need to do that.

Events are ongoing, and you never really finish with them because they are your "stuff." If something is painful for you at the time, we guarantee that later you will encounter a situation that is similar, and you will have gained a compassion that you never had before. You will see the situation all in a different perspective.

What is coming up now are the things that originally blocked you from perceiving reality. These are the parts of your emotional body in which the highway system was severed and the information could not flow, so you moved into pain and translated the emotional pain out of your physical body. We recommend to all of you that you receive bodywork. Bodywork simply involves bringing energy from outside the cosmos into your body, infusing it with your other bodies—mental, physical, emotional, and spiritual—and making the energy grid fit. Where the energy grid fits and you don't block cellular memory and you allow energy to step into your body, the energy moves through your chakras and feeds your body its data. When you are afraid or you shut down, or when you blame someone else, or when you are in denial, you get stuck. Then, even though light floods into your body, it does not fit with the gridwork. So you are in chaos, and everybody else wants to stay away from you because you emanate chaos. Chaos is a fine place to be; there is nothing wrong with chaos as long as you don't permanently dwell there.

When you deny emotion, you are asking for major Earth changes to take place within your psyche. When you allow a tornado here, a hurricane there, or a small volcanic eruption here and there, you are allowing your emotions freedom of expression, and they will not run rampant over your personal environment.

Feeling is what connects you to your humanity; feeling is what connects you to your emotions. Emotions connect you in this realm of existence to your spiritual body. What we are saying is that emotions, or feelings, are the key to being alive in this reality. Many realities exist without emotions, but in this reality they are your greatest gift. If you deny your emotional self in this lifetime, then you had best realize that you have hung it up. If you are not going to be part of your emotional self, then you are never going to make the game we are talking about. You will simply be one of the masses who watches television and feels like a victim over and over again. If you are feeling pain within your emotional body, ask yourself why you believe the pain is there, what purpose the pain serves, and why you are choosing to create pain through your emotions. Why is it not your choice to create joy? *All is choice.* We need to remind you of this.

FIFTEEN

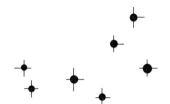

Earth's Initiation Through Integrity

This beautiful Earth is a treasure so profound and so mag-
nanimous that it draws those from far in space to come cherish
the beauty that is here. We want you to feel that beauty inside
yourselves and let it pulsate within your own beings. As you
allow this beauty to come into you, it will move you profoundly,
and you will begin as a species to command that the beautifica-
tion of Earth become the first priority for all. We want to seed this
idea into you so that you awaken to your responsibility to Earth.
We have awakened within you the responsibility to yourselves,
and you are on the road to becoming the best that you can be; we
congratulate you. Now, what are you going to do for Earth, and
how are you going to do it?

We have taught you to command the best for yourself in all
possible moments. Since Earth is your home, how are you now
going to extend this energy to Earth and affect this planet with
what you know?

How many of you have walked your own property, consid-
ering it a sacred space, and let Earth know how much you
treasure it? That sort of communication will get you involved
with the beautiful Earth. *Involve yourselves in doing.* Look at your
garbage, at what you are throwing away, and at what you are
unconscious of. It is an exact reflection of what we have asked
you to do with yourselves. Look at your thoughts and at the
garbage that clutters your psyche. All we have taught you, you

can extend to Earth. Wherever you go, communicate with Earth and let the planet know you are awakening. You must think of yourself as a thread of light; wherever you walk, drive, fly, or visit, you are carrying your thread of light. As more and more threads are woven around the planet, eventually there will be a fantastic cosmic wave of light.

We are in a world that is on the brink of slowing down before it goes into a mad frenzy. You can begin that slowdown by consciously taking greater care of Earth. The predominant consciousness on Earth at this time, particularly in the United States, maintains that having the best-looking lawn is a status symbol. In order to have that best-looking lawn, you use as many pesticides and chemical fertilizers as possible until the lawn begins to look like a carpet that would be in your living room. Where did that value system come from, and what is the sense in it? The sense in that value system is that someone made money off a product and created a marketing campaign that gave that product legitimacy, and someone bought it.

Communicate with Earth, listen to it, and let this beautiful planet teach you how to live in harmony. This is a slow process, and you are not going to learn it overnight. Hear Earth saying, "Listen, would you like someone pouring pesticides on your skin?" This is what happens when you pour them on Earth. Earth is a sentient being, or collection of beings. The sentient beings that make up Earth came into this collective of consciousness out of love for the unity of this consciousness and desire to experience being a home for consciousness. This is like you being the home for all the bacteria and all the things that live on your skin and inside your body. You work with them. Earth understands that, in order to be a good mother to its children, it must let the children learn their own lessons. Your lessons are, of course, the lessons of responsibility. If you want something, there are certain ramifications and things you must do and re-sponsibilities you must take on to accomplish your goal. Earth is teaching human beings responsibility by allowing you to create disruption upon its surface and into its interior.

When Earth is in jeopardy and humanity has pushed things too far, Earth will do whatever is necessary to teach the human species about the proper care of its home, in order for you as the inhabitants to learn a bigger lesson. In divine love of humanity and divine acceptance of its role as teacher, Earth will teach you about its own secrets and power so that you can understand how to walk with cooperation and love of Earth and not walk with disrespect.

This inevitably leads to the overwhelming probability of Earth doing some major changes in order to capture the consciousness of human beings and point out to them what they are missing. If twenty million people disappeared in an afternoon because of an Earth change, perhaps the other humans would wake up. *Perhaps.*

You have heard the predictions of Earth changes over and over again. Some of you have taken them with a grain of salt. You have not thought they would happen to you, though you might think they would happen to someone else or in the newspaper halfway around the world. What about when a change happens at your doorstep or in the next city over? What about when the major cities in the United States begin to collapse? How do you think you will feel if you awake someday and find that there has been a tear in the Earth from New York City to Washington, D.C.? Would that be enough to shake you up a little bit? Enough to restructure and revalue your lives?

You are becoming more aware of what is going on because now your newspapers are beginning to carry the stories. The stories have actually been there for some time. There have been environmentalists and conservationists talking about environmental changes for twenty years, but people figured that the problems would fix themselves. Besides, environmental issues do not sell newspapers, and, to a certain extent, people have not been interested in learning about responsibility. That attitude is going to backfire; most people will claim ignorance and think the issues came out of nowhere. Things are going to get so severe that we predict there will be countries that will ban the use of the automobile.

Earth's teachings or lessons at this time have to do with many things. As frequencies change, everything changes. When frequencies change, it is like moving from your house: the whole environment changes. These changes are designed to uplift everyone's life. They are designed to bring everyone to a greater place of ease and comprehension. They are designed to disengage human beings from the paradigm that has defined your world as solid and in very limited terms.

When human beings make quality of life the number one priority in their lives by honoring the quality of Earth's life, there will be very few Earth changes upon this planet. However, most humans, particularly in the Western world, are concerned with a very different quality of life: how many electronic devices they own, how many clothes are in their closets, and how many cars are in their garages. They are not at all connected to the effects of all of this material manufacturing on the sentient being that is your parent.

If human beings do not change—if they do not make the shift in values and realize that without Earth they could not be here—then Earth, in its love for its own initiation and its reaching for a higher frequency, will bring about a cleansing that will balance it once again. There is the potential for many people to leave the planet in an afternoon. Maybe then everyone else will begin to wake up to what is going on. There have been events all along stimulating you, encouraging you, and bringing you to the realization that there must be global change. There are grass-roots movements that are going to grow phenomenally. What happens to Earth depends on how willing everyone is to change.

What is *your* responsibility in this? How willing are you to change? The time has come not to just talk about it but to *do it*. As you commit to change in your own life, you automatically make the change available to the entire planet.

Earth is striving for its integrity. The planet feels at this time deprived of its integrity, dishonored, and unloved. Earth loves you and gives you a place to operate; it is a living organism. Earth is about to reestablish its integrity and let you understand the importance of loving yourself by loving Earth. Love yourself and love Earth, because they are the same.

Earth changes could play an important role in breaking down the system. They will bring about the collapse of the insurance companies, which will bring about the collapse of many other systems. Many of the banking businesses sell their mortgages to the insurance companies, and the insurance companies invested very heavily in the junk-bond industry. Given a few more major disasters like Hurricane Hugo or the San Francisco earthquake coupled with war and the underground economy—how long do you think they can continue to operate? On paper, no one has quite caught up with this yet. It is still a matter of checks shuffling from one bank to another and keeping everything just above water. So Earth changes, more than likely, will be utilized in some way to bring about that collapse. Earth changes will also bring about a joining and triumph of the human spirit because men and women will go out to help other men and women when disasters occur. This bonds people.

There are technologies that could clean this place up very quickly if that were the plan. However, as the species at present does not take responsibility for Earth, there would be no point. The present species must learn to honor its nest. All of you must learn to honor your bodies because without your bodies you would not be here, and without Earth you would not be here. Your body and your planet are your two greatest gifts and the most valuable things you own. Ideally, you would express a sacredness and honoring and cherishing and love of Earth and your physical being. This would resonate in your home, your property, the land you are associated with, and the land of your body as well.

Earth is more resilient than you would imagine. It is here to feed you and sustain you. The animals are also here to work in cooperation with you. If everything is done with love, it has the force of the Creator behind it. Done with love, there would be no hurt and no harm. If you need a guide to make decisions about your behavior, ask yourself: "Am I operating with my highest integrity? Am I operating with love? Is love my intention for Earth, the animals, all the people I encounter, and all the things I do?"

Everything of Earth can be used if Earth is loved and honored in the process. It may be difficult to imagine a gang of oil workers, before they set the bit into the ground, holding hands and asking for guidance and permission to penetrate Earth. Yet, if this were done, things would be much more in harmony. You laugh because you deem it foolishness to communicate to something that does not talk back. But if industry, educators, and all people first stopped and committed to the highest integrity and love for all involved and asked that there be no harm to Earth or humans, it would be phenomenally received. This would put into motion the plan for a high civilization. Such awareness is beginning to come; many people are getting this kind of information at this time.

Many human beings do not want to put themselves on the line and stand up in integrity because they are afraid of getting into trouble. They say, "I will just keep my job and my security; what the heck." One of the most incredible things that can happen in any society occurs when everyone's security is taken away. Courage begins to blossom like a freshly planted garden because people have nothing to lose. Humans begin to stand up.

Never feel that your efforts are in vain. Use the power of your mind to clearly intend what you want. Ask for assistance from the nonphysical realms and visualize the outcome you would like to have. Understand that you create your reality and that every other person creates their reality. Everyone has the opportunity to wake up at any time. When you approach anything, approach it from the bigger picture.

When enough people create their own reality—*consciously create it*—you will create a new planet. There will literally be a splitting of worlds. This splitting will more than likely not occur for more than twenty years. In the meantime, Earth will more than likely be ravaged by war quite a few times. You will have some very puzzling and confusing space dramas take place with some space cousins who need to figure out quite publicly who they are.

Earth is on a dimensional collision course, and many dimensions or probabilities will intersect one another in this decade. Some of these realities will be shocking, depending upon the level of shock each person needs to kick their consciousness into another paradigm. Shock does not mean destruction, necessarily. It can simply be a method to alter the way you view reality. Whenever you are shocked by something, you can no longer grip reality the way you gripped it the moment before. There is an instantaneous kick in the stomach, and everything changes. The world is in for numerous shocks, and not simply on a national level. We are talking about global intersections of dimensions by which realities will seem to come tumbling down only for those whose realities need to crumble.

The concept of probabilities maintains that there is no one reality and that you, yourselves, branch off into other realities continuously through your thoughts. It is not that you change the world, it is that you change which world you occupy. This goes back to the idea that the world is not solid. It is constructed of energy, and that energy takes form through the thoughts of those that participate within the world.

There are, and there always have been, probable Earths and probable experiences. There are probable "you's" leading quite different lives than the *you* you know. You are frequency and energy. You are pulsating to the beat of a chord of energy that sings you into existence, and you are so familiar with it that you stay focused continuously on one aspect of your experience. Experience is gained from many perspectives, and you are learning how to change the frequency and beat so that you can notice what you usually do not notice.

You are continuously monitored as to the effect of the neurological changes that are taking place in your bodies. The rewiring or restructuring is like your nervous system going from a two-lane highway system to a twelve-lane highway system. When this takes place, you will have memories of events that have run simultaneously with other events. At first, this may freak you out a little bit because you will have no place to plug them in.

For example, say two years down the road you remember a Thanksgiving dinner you had in 1989 or 1990. Then suddenly, you have a memory of an event you never before remembered, and it is right next to and parallel to the Thanksgiving dinner you *did* remember. You then realize that you were at two Thanksgivings. This is what will happen as the nervous system comes into a new pulsation and the body has its library put back together. As the light-encoded filaments reform themselves and broadcast what they have available, the nervous system must be able to carry and translate it.

There is a great polarization of energies occurring, with many participants and observers. Many who have come to observe have come to disrupt as well; they have come to learn their "stuff" in this time. There are also participants who are completely intent on creating a world that will be quite glorious. As we see it, as the probable worlds begin to form, there will be great shiftings within humanity on this planet. It will seem that great chaos and turmoil are forming, that nations are rising against each other in war, and that earthquakes are happening more frequently. It will seem as if everything is falling apart and cannot be put back together. Just as you sometimes have rumblings and quakings in your lives as you change your old patterns and move into new energies, Earth is shaking itself free, and a certain realignment or adjustment period is to be expected. It will also seem that the animals and fish are departing Earth. Those animals are now moving over to the new world as it is being formed. They are not ending their existence, they are merely slipping into the new world to await your joining them.

It is difficult to explain this, to a certain extent, because it is beyond the third-dimensional experience. Basically, you are moving into the fourth dimension. When this move is made, you will literally form a new Earth. It will seem as if you have awoken from a dream into a world that is pristine and beautiful. Your skies are full of observers watching and waiting to see how you will do this and offering to give you assistance in doing it. For many people, it seems as if this shift is completely beyond all possibility. But not for you who have studied this energy as alchemists and ancient Atlanteans in temple life. The training you have had in other times is encoded within your beings to prepare you for this juncture.

The people who leave the planet during the time of Earth changes do not fit here any longer, and they are stopping the harmony of Earth. When the time comes that perhaps twenty million people leave the planet at one time, there will be a tremendous shift in consciousness for those who are remaining. When a large group passes over together, they create an impact upon the consciousness of those who remain.

Expand yourselves. Begin to dwell in other realities besides the reality that is work and sleep and eating. When you are awake, let your mind expand to possibilities and let ideas come to you. Ideas are free; they are everywhere, and there are broadcasts continuously coming to the planet.

When Earth does its shifting, not everyone will experience the same thing. Those who need to experience destruction will experience an Earth shift or rotation with destruction because they will not fit with the new frequency. Those who are prepared to hold a higher vibration will experience a frequency shift. So for one person there may be the end of their life as they know it and dire destruction, while for another there will be a state of ecstasy. All potentials exist. Remember, you live in a symbolic world that is a result of your thoughts. The outside world represents to you what is going on internally with you. So if the world is falling apart, what does that represent? It represents the falling apart or collapsing of what is inside in order to create the rise of a new system and a new energy.

It is imperative for you to love and bless the changes within

society and not move into fear or anxiety about what is present-
ing itself. It is your task to be in the vibration of knowing, even
without sense, that in every event there is an opportunity for
Spirit to do its work and to uplift. You are an exceptionally lazy
species. You give your power away to anyone who will do
things for you, whether it is your boss or your wife or husband.
You give your power away over and over again. In order to turn
you toward yourselves, you need some events to put you in
charge of your lives. Bless these changes that come to Earth and,
in these events, trust that what you want with clarity will be
manifest. You will find yourself tested. You will say, "Am I a
victim here? Is the world collapsing around me? Or is it uplifting itself around me while everything is seemingly in the midst
of collapse?"

An important primary belief for you to hold is that you will
be in the right place at the right time doing the right thing.
Intending that you will be in the right place at the right time—
more than intending it, *knowing it*—will open you to guidance.
Perhaps without even looking for it, a piece of land or an opportunity to connect with someone else will be put before you.
You will recognize it and say, "This is for me. I shall take this."

Believe it or not, there will come a time—or let us say, there
could come a time—in many of your lives when you will shut the
door on life as you now know it. Literally, you may give up the
house that you have and walk out of it with only a few possessions. It does not seem possible now, does it? Something
inside of you will say, "My God, has the world gone mad? What
are my values? What is the most important thing now for my
survival?" And Spirit will come in and guide you to tell you
what is the most important thing for your survival. That may
mean simply carting off a few possessions. Some of you in this
life will literally stand on the threshold of your houses, look
within, and it will all be meaningless because the most important things will be your spiritual values and your life. All those
material possessions and collections of things mean nothing in
light of what you are becoming. Can you imagine the events that

will be needed to move you to that action? They are not going to be small events.

Remember humanity's destiny to evolve. We guarantee that life as you now know it will not be around ten years from now. The world as you know it, the reality as you know it, the comforts and projections and vacations and all the things that you do will not be here ten years from now. You are here for your own personal evolution. How that evolution is going to come about worldwide will be rather interesting. We are not talking about the evolution of a few dozen people; we are talking about the evolution of the species. There will need to be some events to bring people to awakening. That is why it is going to be your challenge to live your life with courage and to have the courage to live your light.

We recommend that all of you intend that the Native American teachings come your way. Begin to explore them through sweatlodges, drumming, dancing, and so on. This will awaken many things in you and teach you much about Earth. You are coded to ritual; when you perform ritual, your body begins to remember who you are and what you know.

As we see it, communities are going to be very influential in the 1990s. They will form on tracts of land that will be anywhere from fifty to a few hundred acres, perhaps as small as twenty-five acres, and they may house anywhere from thirty to one hundred people. These groups will come together because the members will be responding to an inner knowing. The new technologies that will be used in the coming communities will be technologies based on love. There is nothing wrong with technology. The major stumbling block of technology now in use on this planet is that it is used to separate, manipulate, and control people rather than to uplift them. Technology with love is the key. Many people will be given great amounts of technological information that will seemingly come out of nowhere. You may be given information for an invention and yet not have any idea what it is you are inventing. You may have to hand it over to someone else to bring it into reality. People will work together in harmony to bring forth this new technology.

Part of the evolution of consciousness involves uniting one consciousness with another—not keeping yourselves separated. Perhaps one person will come up with an idea, and another one will take the idea and put it into manifestation, and someone else will sell it. As we see it, there will be a tremendous underground market for inventions. These inventions will never be shown in the traditional marketplace because you would be wiped out, snuffed, if it was known that you had these abilities. There will be great trading from one community to another of these underground technologies that will do all kinds of things for you.

It can be one of the most rewarding experiences of this lifetime for you to live in cooperation with a group of people who love the land and get the land—Earth—to respond. In loving the land and letting Earth know what you are after, Earth will nurture and take care of you. That is the key.

SIXTEEN

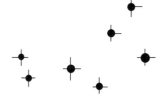

Heretics Ahead of Time

The sixties were a time of preparation. They held your initial awakening and were a time that showed you that new paradigms could be born. During that decade, you suddenly became far removed from the values of the previous generations. The sixties were full of events, such as the movement for peace and the movement for expression of the body, which supported looking at the body and accepting and sharing sexuality with full consciousness—with clothes off, rather than by finding body parts between layers of clothes, which is what the generation before did. Consciousness was birthed, and the idea of peace and freedom was awakened. That was kindergarten.

The nineties are the time to bring the movement of spirituality onto the planet—not just in small pockets, but onto the entire planet. The planet is awakening all over. We travel the planet and can tell you that you have your counterparts in every corner of the globe. The team of light that you represent made sure that they covered all their bases, because there are lightworkers everywhere. You are coming into your own.

The movement toward spirituality is a movement away from materialism. Over the last number of years, many people have gotten very into their bodies, regenerating them, exercising them, and making them more beautiful. That has simply been preparation so that you could move into Spirit. The realm of Spirit is a very exciting place. It has more flexibility: there are places to travel and great adventures to be had, and there are no limitations.

The reason physical reality has been so frustrating for you is because you bought the stories about its limitations hook, line, and sinker. You bought them because you had made an agreement to do so. It was part of your plan to buy into these limitations so that you could relate to those who have no idea about light and who have been buying into the limitations for their whole existence. You are going to electromagnetically alter the planet—rewire it, so to speak—so that all of these other beings can be plugged in once again. You can only do this if you can relate to where they are.

If you had come here with your memory banks open, either you would not have wanted to stay or you would not now understand the others. So you have been submerged in a society that has been without light, and you have forgotten your light (or vaguely remembered it as you grew up) so that you could relate to that world. Now it is time for you to integrate that world of society into the multidimensional world of light and Spirit you represent so that the values and designs of this planet will begin to change completely.

Heretics are ahead of their time. The heretical ideas that come onto the planet always prove to be brilliant later. So have courage; it only seems as if these new ideas are being ridiculed. You must remember that there is much activity in the nonphysical realms to assist you and that, even though each of you has your own blueprint and plan to evolve into, you are part of a global blueprint and a global consciousness. You are firing that global blueprint and awakening others.

You awaken in waves as each of you learns to carry information and broadcast it. If everyone were awakened at once, it would be very chaotic. The awakening must happen as you are able to handle it, because putting too much light into an element that cannot handle it would blow a fuse. If the electrical currents are not matched up, the body can be destroyed. You will see this. You are going to see a disease move over the planet that has to do with the nervous system and memory because people won't be able to handle the energy. They will become frightened of it. They may discover a multidimensional portion of themselves and think they are crazy. Then they will be obsessed with keeping their insanity quiet from their husband or wife or children. People will drive themselves into a frenzy with this energy because they won't understand it.

We cannot emphasize enough that the nervous system is the key to open your ancient eyes and see, and for you to remember who you are, where you come from, and where you are going. The nervous system must be able to take the electrical current into the body, transduce the high energy and fit it inside the body, and let the body evolve and nurture itself on this high energy that is consciousness. This is literally what is occurring.

It is as if you were to take a newborn babe and feed this babe a formula that would force it to grow from a day-old infant to a thirty-year-old adult in one year. This parallels what will be happening for you over the next twenty years. That newborn child would become thirty in one year. Think about what that child would have to do and what its body would have to integrate to grow like that. Think about the organs, the functions, and the hormones.

Since you are committed carriers of light, there is a certain opening within your auric field. There is an opening that the pillar of light brings so that guardians can come down and act as gate keepers for how much energy you can handle. Even though your intellect, mind, and ego may say, "More, more, more," the gate keepers know that, because you are a carrier of light and have committed to a certain task, you cannot be lost. Unless, that is, you are bent on your own personal destruction and you move past what is called the highest will into the will of yourself.

The nervous system, which is a highway within the body, can only move at the rate you can process the data flooding over it into the cells. Many of you are still cleaning out caverns within portions of your being that have been filled with darkness. These caverns may be from this lifetime—they may go back to childhood—or for some of you they may be from other lifetimes. Many of you have been on this journey for twenty-five or thirty years, while others of you have newly joined the journey. Not everyone is going to take the same amount of time. Those who have been plodding along for thirty years are way showers. You set up a vibrational frequency that those of you who are new joiners can feel. You who are new joiners don't have to go looking for the new frequency and discover it; the mapping is done, and the mapping hits your body.

You all need one another. It is imperative that you work in harmony. If you don't work in harmony, you will create Atlantis and all of the other destructions over and over again. *Harmony is required.*

A time is coming when many of you will be put to work with Spirit to broadcast frequency and assist others in comprehending what is going on. The waves of awakening will continue, and Spirit will become a way of being on this planet. That is the plan for this planet, and the creative cosmic rays from Prime Creator are hitting the fringes of your galactic system—moving here first. That is why the great gathering of energies has come here. These energies want to participate in the transformation here so that they will be prepared when it comes to their own area of galactic and universal existence.

There is a huge transformation taking place, but what you do with it, of course, is up to you. We have said that your world is going to split into two worlds and that those who move with light will be in the world of light. This split is already beginning to take place. Those entities who wish to work with the higher vibratory fields that represent light, and those who wish to work with the lower vibratory fields that represent fear, darkness, chaos, control, and confusion, are beginning to polarize and choose sides.

Those who work with the lower vibratory fields will say to you that you are witches or the devil because you represent something that they don't understand. You represent change, and you must remember that most people are frightened to death of change. One of the curious things about human consciousness is that it is enamored of stability. You bought the concept that stability is something desirable hook, line, and sinker. So you strive for it; you think that if you do not have stability and security then who are you? You might not exist, you might be annihilated.

We are talking about many people you know; some may even be family members. You will need to develop a tremendous amount of patience and compassion for those who feel this energy and do not want to respond to it in a way that can benefit them. You are going to have to become very allowing—perhaps even allowing others to destroy themselves so that they can learn the value of life.

Even though human beings are not consciously aware of it, you know in the deepest portion of your beings that you move from one existence to another and gather experience so that your soul can understand and process data to give you a view of one reality. Someday you will be able to scan the lives and existences of your soul and hold the energy of that soul just like you would hold a crystal, look at the different facets and sparkles within it, and feel and know that identity. When you are able to do this with your soul, your soul will be able to connect with other forms of intelligence that it is a part of but does not presently comprehend.

We are stretching you. We want you to become completely confused so that you will be energized. Then you will utilize your curiosity to take you into areas that, not only have you never thought of, you never even knew existed. This is our intention—that you come to a higher ground where you can create a new order of identity *courageously, with humor, and with confidence.*

All things are frequencies. If you knew how rapidly you are evolving, you might want to sit in a chair and put your hand over your head and say, "I can't do it. There is too much going on for me." You keep the veil pulled down and pretend to go about life as if nothing is happening when you are continuously being upgraded with all kinds of changes to bring you closer to the higher dimensions. Think about and feel what you are going to achieve in one lifetime. Within the next ten to twenty years, you will move from being dense physical creatures into creatures of light in the Age of Light. Can you conceive of this?

Everything that you are doing, including eating a pizza, is bringing you in a divinely perfect way to that place. At some point you will understand the importance of every event in which you are participating and the integrity of the whole.

In the movie *The Karate Kid*, the kid is very impatient while learning karate. He finds a master and doesn't even think he has found a master. He is given things to do that he thinks are a waste of time. He does not understand that each piece he learns makes up the greater whole. You are like this kid. All the pieces are coming together, but because of the vision of your ego, you do not understand at this time that they make the greater whole. You will be put to task, and you will find that all you are seeking will be yours. That is the good news.

Be aware and learn how to recognize when your will is usurping the divine will and the Divine Plan—when you are forcing too much onto yourself because you are not operating out of common sense. Look at yourself in the mirror and see how you look. Look into your eyes because your eyes are an indicator for your whole physical body. Are they clear? Are you able to look back with clarity? Is your face lined, or exhausted, or calm? How does your body feel? Are you able to sit in a serene position? Are you able to hold your body erect, or do you feel the need to slump over? Do you fidget because you cannot hold the energy in your body—so your body is always dancing and twitching because it does not know what to do? Are your fingers always drumming, or are you gnawing at your flesh? There are many indications to watch for. You can look around and see who cannot integrate energy.

Once you bring this energy into your body and are able to

hold it, your body will begin to feel a lightness. There will be a vitality in your skin, or perhaps your hair. Your hair is a very good indication of your health. Common sense, of course, is one of your best comrades to hang around with. Common sense will show you what is right and what is not.

At times you will recognize that the energy has become too much and that you are not calm and centered. This will occur for each and every one of you at some point. In some way, you will feel as if too much is happening: there will be too much data to compute, too many people to talk to, or too much going on. When this happens, you must think of yourself as an appliance and unplug yourself. Just like you are a toaster, simply unplug yourself so that you can be out of use. At those times, what you need to do more than anything else is rest. Some of you will need a tremendous amount of sleep at different points. Do not think you are getting lazy and beat up on yourself; simply acknowledge it. There will be times when some of you will wish to sleep eighteen hours. *Do it.* It is necessary. You have no idea of the lands you travel to and the work done on your physical body when you sleep. It is the time when you are unplugged from this reality and recharged and taught in other realities. The bridges, and your eyes, will open between realities, and you will begin to see and carry these memories.

When you go to a Chinese restaurant, you eat Chinese food; you don't order a hamburger. When you go to an Italian restaurant, you order lasagna. This restaurant called Earth has a physical body, so that is how you must operate here—*within a physical body.*

We speak in very simple terms so that you will get our point. It doesn't make any difference how ridiculous our metaphor is, we simply want you to get it. So you are here in the restaurant of Earth, occupying an Earth body because this is what is available here. There is nothing else served up here. You are going to bring new recipes into the Earth restaurant—recipes that periodically have been tested and proven true, but only in pockets here and there.

Remember, Earth was sealed off eons ago. Earth was created to be one thing and then completely got off track after millions of years of existence. Many of you incarnated here over and over again and got really frustrated, because every time you incarnated you had an intention of doing something, but half the time you forgot what it was.

Some of you were able to achieve mastery upon this planet and get yourselves off it through the ascension process. Others of you clamored that you wanted a time when this quarantine or seclusion from the rest of cosmic society would come to an end. Because of you and the multitudes that are upon this planet and surrounding this planet, the present time period was born.

Assistance comes to you in all avenues of life, yet others cannot do things for you because you designed life in such a way that the species must self-motivate and evolve in order to be empowered. Those of you who are tremendously knowledgeable decided to incarnate in the species to empower it by being an example for the rest who cannot do it for themselves. You make new pathways of being as you broadcast who you are. When you gather in rooms for channelings, you ask for a tremendous number of reminders and a tremendous amount of encouragement along the way. Some of you are finding that you cannot make it without the encouragement. This is understood. It is why we are here, most of the time with tremendous patience, for you. We wish to give you the opportunity to claim who you are.

One of the most important ultimate realities upon this planet for you as a species to understand, and one of the greatest challenges you have been faced with, is what it means to die. We can convince you of many things, but it is difficult for us to convince you that you do not have to die. In this time, you do not have to physically leave your body behind here upon this planet. Can you conceive of the idea that you will simply change the vibrational rate of your physical being and take your body with you because you will rearrange the molecular structure?

Making the ascension leap and completing the journey here is possible for a multitude of the species upon this planet. Some of you have already ascended off this planet, and you have come back to do it again and to show the way. It was a grand journey to get out of here with the ascension process. It took lifetimes of training, one after another, to bring yourself to dedication. It involved not living in the material society and basically living very close to nature to do it.

Now those of you who have done this and are familiar with it have come back. It is your goal to ascend off this planet and to be taken, literally, up into the higher cosmology of mother ships. You will ascend into the cities of light and be able to dwell within the other realities that are all around you that you simply do not permit your third-dimensional eyes to see. You will have completed your task on Earth, and Earth will make its transition. It will be a beautiful jewel in the universe. You may wish to stay for some years to help with the restructuring and re-building of this new Earth. But after a while, you will want to move on to new assignments to transform other worlds. Remember, you are renegades, and you like a very exciting time. So most likely you will leave this beautiful planet to others to enjoy, and you will go on to a new assignment.

Ascension is the goal on this planet. There will come a time when that will be the only way people who live on this planet will depart from it. Once you get off this planet, you will go to many other places. You will show yourself and the rest of the species that the body, this thing that seems so solid and uncontrollable, is actually a result of a divine orchestration, and that you, in your consciousness, can do anything you want with it. *Anything.*

SEVENTEEN

The Language of Light

The avatars and masters have now permeated the gridwork of the world, bringing with them their own tools for teaching. The tools that are being utilized on this planet are artifacts that are not of your dimension, symbolic forms that literally have a life of their own. They make up what is known as the Language of Light.

You are implanted with a structure, a geometric form, which triggers certain information within you. It also facilitates, for those who work with you, the sending of information directly into your being. The large majority of you are implanted, and, if you are not now, shortly you will be if you choose to open and align yourself. No one is implanted who does not choose it. This structure of the Language of Light is a way of receiving information and energy to facilitate your development. It is a method of learning without doing it through books or through the intellect. It involves opening to the belief that there is indeed a hierarchy, immense beyond your comprehension, that has been working with humanity since the very beginning.

This hierarchy works with love, cherishes who you are, and has been able to see through the time mechanisms that are keyed into the planet to know that consciousness is ready for the evolutionary leap. There are 144,000 members of the spiritual hierarchy who are infused in the gridwork of the planet at this time. Each master has its own seal that represents one portion of the Language of Light, and you have 144,000 seals of energy that will eventually be infused within your being.

To start with, you will work with the twelve forms that the body will be able to hold. Much later, once the transformation has occurred, there will be an infusion of the entire 144,000 symbolic language structures through your being. That will be an unfoldment that cannot even be explained in this lifetime.

This mutation is a process unfolding within you that will allow you to move into another realm of experience. Each person on the planet has the potential to move through this mutation. Many will stop the process because they do not have the desire to align themselves with higher consciousness. When you are aware of who you are, that is one thing. When you become aware of the divine consciousness that seeds this planet—an intellect that is vast, loving, and works with you—and when you call to that consciousness and ask to be a portion of it, that is when you are implanted with the geometric forms.

The forms that are implanted come in a variety of shapes such as the pyramid structure. Why is the pyramid so important? On this planet and throughout the cosmos, the pyramid structure is utilized to represent a great unity of consciousness. It is the structure that is the most difficult to create in all of its many facets, and yet it is a structure of perfection. It is a structure that gathers energy from Earth and sends it outward.

The structures of the sphere and the spiral will also be implanted inside you. The spiral is very dear to many of you because you have sojourned within cultures and societies where the spiral was utilized to communicate many ideas. There will also be implanted the structures of the parallel lines and the cube. And, of course, there will be the structure of the Merkabah vehicle, which is the five-sided figure.

The five-sided figure represents the figure of the human being in its most unlimited state—the totally free human. Some of you know it as a symbolic structure called a Merkabah vehicle. It is the human design without any limitations. It is the human being able to fly, which is something that a large majority of you do not think you can do. This implant comes when you truly commit yourself to what was formerly not possible.

Which implant or geometric form will be implanted inside you will depend first of all on your request for alignment. It will also depend on your belief that these entities choose to be available to you if you choose to be available for them. As you begin to unfold and allow what are called miracles or magnificent events to manifest in your life, they will begin.

Many of you will start with the implant of the circle because it represents God-form, unity, and completeness. Some of you will select the pyramid structure to be implanted since you have had many lifetimes with discovered and still undiscovered pyramids all over the planet. You think your geography is known, but there are many things still undiscovered because they are slipping from one reality to another. Deep within jungles, there are many buried pyramids, often lying buried beneath mounds of earth. There are still many wonders to uncover.

Those of you who are willing to believe that there are truly no limitations will be able to take the Merkabah structure and move yourself off the planet with it while you are still living on the planet. The desire to do this must exist in you if you are to be implanted with the Merkabah. Already some of you have attempted to travel with it, and you know how it can be used in your being. When you truly call the Merkabah to yourself, and you are willing to get the feeling of what that truly means—to be unlimited consciousness that travels with your body, without your body leaving the planet—that is when implanting will occur. The Merkabah is not the highest implanting, as there are no highest or lowest implantings. Implanting comes when it will best suit your personal development. Once you have become implanted, there will be an unending process of new forms coming into your being.

You do not consciously choose the form that will be implanted in you. However, you choose the life you have, which opens you to the structures of the Language of Light. You choose what is important to you each day. That is your access to these forms. Through this marriage of energies, eventually you will all hold the alphabet of light inside your beings, and this alphabet of light will teach you. If you have dreamt of geometric forms, it is an indication that the forms are working with you. Or perhaps you loved studying geometry in school. If you wish to know what you have been implanted with, see which forms continuously come first or are larger than the others. There are many shapes that do not even have names. There will be shapes that you know and recognize that later will take new forms and new shapes that your consciousness cannot translate.

The spiral is one of the basic forms of the Language of Light geometry. It is a bridge, a teaching unto itself. The form of it is coded with information, and when you ride the spiral, it is seemingly nonending. This shows you that the journey into your self is nonending and that the journey outside of yourself is nonending. You, as a species, will be able to split your consciousness and go in both directions so that consciousness can be connected. By taking the nonending journey within and the nonending journey without, you link yourself up into a connected spiral in which there is universal truth.

We have said that the cells in your body contain the entire history of this universe. Ideally, you will come to realize the existence of this golden library within yourselves during this lifetime and learn how to read what is there. Taking the spiral within is one part of the journey. The trick is to both go within and go without—and to realize that they are the same.

The spiral exists in many dimensions. When you visualize the spiral, you will feel that you have known it, yet at first you are only knowing one aspect of it. When you begin to grow with the spiral, you will realize that it has so many dimensions that you could spend the rest of eternity—to use your term— exploring it. It grows. The spiral is the key to tapping into what is inside of you. Your DNA is in the form of a spiral. Spirals are all around you, and the Language of Light rides upon the light-encoded filaments that also descend in spiral form. This is something that is experiential, and it will grow for you.

In your meditation, feel yourself riding a spiral like you would ride a tornado. Visualize yourself seeing a spiral approaching that is like a tornado. Then, instead of running from it, stand there and feel yourself whirled up inside of it. Ride it, for it is a doorway to other realities.

These Language of Light geometrical shapes and forms are collections of experiences of individuals who have incarnated on this planet, defied the human laws, awakened themselves to high abilities and then manifested themselves as language and geometric components. Once these energies existed as men and women on this planet. They have evolved themselves into geometric symbols, and they exist in their sphere of activity just like you exist in your body. These entities exist in a language system or a geometric system.

There are universes of these systems, and there are visitations into your own universe from those universes at this time. There are circles and other shapes being put upon this planet in the grain fields that are inexplicable as far as you are concerned. These imprints are a frequency, not a process or action. There is a song or story or language that is being implanted on the surface of Earth with language symbols. These symbols come to establish a certain frequency, and they are going to increase.

Eventually, some of you will build houses that are geometric shapes that are not simply squares or rectangles. Many of the dwellings in the Pleiades do not have shapes as you know them, and it is understood there that shapes and angles hold energy. In astrology, it is understood that certain angles have power points and that certain things happen with certain angles. It is the same with shapes. The Great Pyramid is all about the use of angles and shapes. Energy collects in angles, in shapes, and in forms, and you can learn to create these shapes and live in and around them. Energies are formed and transmitted in this way. You will also discover that certain degrees have certain powers, and that some angles are very uncomfortable for you to be in. It is sometimes better to sleep in the middle of a room rather than having your bed jammed into a ninety-degree angle, because the ninety-degree angle creates an energy lock. In the middle of the room, the energy flows around you.

In third-dimensional reality, many portals are now being opened to bring about evolution upon Earth. At one time, the planet was sealed off and put in quarantine because there were forces that fought here. There have been incredible wars upon this planet, and some of the vestiges of these wars still exist as very barren areas upon the planet. This was the time of chaos and confusion when creator gods fought creator gods. During the most recent wave of the wars, about ten or twelve thousand years ago, Earth was sealed off because those beings who operated with light lost the battle. Light does not always win, you know. Light is not always the victor as you think of a victor, for light must learn to integrate with all portions of itself. Prime Creator is within all things, and light and dark are part of the Creator. Therefore, light must incorporate with the dark portion of itself.

Time has orchestrated and brought events together. A number of cycles were set to pass since the last wars, after which time the energy portals into the planet would again be opened so that light could enter. This is that time period. Light is being orchestrated to once again come onto the planet, and it is increasing daily. In order for energy to work its way through your consciousness, it must house itself on the planet. Intelligence penetrates in the form of waves making geometric shapes on Earth. It is not that a spaceship comes down, makes crop circles in the night, and then takes off. Although some circles have been caused by ship landings, intelligence can take the guise of any form it wants, and very often intelligence comes in the form of a wave. A time will come when there will actually be a wave of light that sweeps Earth.

Intelligence is beyond the spoken word and beyond the written word, for it is frequency that sometimes comes in geometric shapes. Pythagoras had a beginning grasp of this, but his geometry was not understood by others. Geometry is an evolved intelligence, a collection of experience that can communicate huge amounts of information. Actually, crop circles all over the planet are put there by sounds above human frequency to implement these language shapes. Many times, in the beginning, these shapes are circles. They will evolve into triangles, lines, and many other things.

The crop circles have been most prevalent in England and throughout Europe. However, they are also in the area previously known as the Soviet Union and in South America. They are even in the United States, although some people are doing a good job of pretending they are not there. We understand that some of your news broadcasters are planning upcoming shows about these crop circles. We will see how much they pretend they don't know about them. It is going to be interesting.

These geometric shapes are like hieroglyphs. The hieroglyphs and pictographs carved in stone on this planet are a similar generation of intelligence. In other words, if one were to read the hieroglyphs based on the Rosetta Stone, the hieroglyphs would communicate one thing. If one were able to remember the secret language of the priests, the hieroglyphs would tell another story. And if one were able to understand the language of the creator gods, they would say something entirely different.

The circles and shapes being put on Earth are here to assist you in holding and managing your frequency and having the courage to live your light. They make frequency information available in a very subtle way, and no one can figure them out yet. These shapes are all connected to one another, and if they were all written out simultaneously on some farmer's field, something would happen to them immediately. They are spaced from one continent to another, and they move a frequency band around the planet that will help activate Earth's gridwork. They will allow you not to feel so weird with what you know and to feel more comfortable with the changes in frequency as they occur.

This is just a little bit of what the crop circles do. They are quite interesting. Many of them are designed and constructed by what some call Ascended Masters. There is also a joke behind them. You must understand that some beings, as they become very evolved, develop a tremendous sense of humor. They see the humor in all things.

As we have said, geometric shapes and forms are carriers of intelligence. They are frequency waves that can be modulated and changed. The shapes coming onto Earth are like energy gates or energy glyphs. They hold intelligence and are being set up to eventually connect and make an intelligent gridwork around the planet. This gridwork will have a frequency that humanity can use to evolve.

The whole language is not on the planet at this time. The glyphs come onto Earth as a result of a certain evolvement of consciousness. They work with places that are vortex centers that are now drawing them in. Over the billions of years that Earth has been in orbit, these centers have been covered over and buried. Some have gone into dormancy, and many of them are being reawakened because the seal around the planet has been penetrated.

The crop circles are phenomenological expressions of consciousness. They come into your reality to show you that the reasoning mind cannot control all of the data, much as it would like to. These events occur to intersect with the coding of consciousness of all human beings. Whenever reality cannot be explained, a certain niche is opened within consciousness. The crop circles are completely beyond the logical mind. Therefore, they force the consensus view of reality to expand, since reality, as formerly designed, cannot house these events as a possibility. They are a trigger. They force reality to move beyond its own limitations.

There are a number of reasons for the existence of the crop circles. Basically, they exist to force reality to move—to get you feeling rather than thinking. Most who explore these circles *think* their way through the circles rather than *feel* their way through them. Great Britain is having a rash of them because, in general, the British have a very logically oriented consciousness. However, the land of the British Isles is imprinted with megalithic spirals and stone forms that have intensely imprinted the intuitive faculties of the inhabitants.

This phenomenon has no logic to it. It is forcing a logically oriented society to recognize something that makes no sense, and it is being done in a very playful and obvious way without creating a threat to anyone's view of reality. If ships were to land everywhere, people would get upset. When corn lies down in concentric circles and doesn't even break or die, no one really gets too upset. Do you understand how energies play with you? It is necessary to do certain things so that you can get it and figure it out without having your circuits overloaded.

This language is being introduced onto the planet as a story—a glyph of information that holds a frequency to assist you in holding your own frequency. As you awaken, it is easy for others to read you and recognize you. You are monitored all of the time, because there are devices that monitor the evolution and location of consciousness. Once consciousness has reached a certain place, assistance is brought from the outside to establish other realms of that frequency.

In other words, say you open a restaurant, and it is a big hit. You run and maintain it and sell really good food. Then someone comes along and says, "How about franchising? Let's get you everywhere." These geometric shapes help you franchise the frequency by spreading it all over the planet and holding it. They bring you to a new level of attainment.

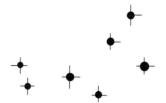

EIGHTEEN

Symphonies of Consciousness

Light informs you. It uplifts you, because once you are informed, you feel more powerful. When you are not informed you feel powerless.

Sound is another way to carry information because it is part of light. To you it may seem that sound and light are two separate things, because from your point of view you perceive light with your eyes and sound with your ears. Because you use two separate areas of perception on your body, it seems that sound and light are separated as well. In actuality, they are very connected. They wind themselves around one another because they both carry information.

Many of the structures built on this planet, particularly ancient sacred sites, have information stored within stone. In the same way, you have information stored within the bones of your skeletal form. When you allow sound to move through you, it unlocks a doorway and allows information to flood into your body. It also penetrates the ground, affecting the vibrations of Earth and allowing a rearrangement of a molecular alignment of information to take place. Those of you who use sound when you are working on others' bodies bring about a rearrangement of the molecular structure and create an opening for information to flood in. This kind of work will become more and more profound.

In Tibet, when a master who was able to transcend realities

passed over, the body was kept and allowed to move into its own natural deterioration because the skeletal form held a sensibility to frequencies. *Information is stored in bone and stone.* In some places in Tibet where the lines of continuity in sects of monks can be traced back for thousands and thousands of years, people have kept the skulls of different masters. They have very secret crypts and rooms filled with these skulls. When one walks into these places, one can, through sound, access the intelligence factors of the humans who once occupied those skulls.

Do you understand why crystal skulls were designed? Crystalline structures are like holographic computers: they can transmit to the evolved or plugged-in human a tremendous amount of information. They are designed like skulls to act as a code for understanding your own skull and understanding that the bone in your body is very valuable.

Sound is a tool for transformation. Keepers of Frequency, which is what we are encouraging you to become, learn how to modulate the frequency they hold through sound. Sound can penetrate any substance, move molecules, and rearrange realities.

In ancient Egypt, the ankh, or symbol that represented life, in actuality was a frequency modulator. It was utilized by individuals who were masters of keeping frequencies and able to do many things with those frequencies. The ankh is similar to a tuning fork and can direct sound. That is how it was used a long time ago. Before you will be able to experience using sound in the manner of the ancient Egyptians, you will have to demonstrate your integrity. You will have to pass an initiation or a testing to see whether you can be trusted with this kind of power. This planet is not ripe for this kind of energy simply to be thrust into anyone's hands. If you were capable of this kind of work at this time, your life would not be safe because there would be too many who would want to misuse your gift. You will be given abilities as you can best mature into them.

You can begin to work with sound by allowing it to "play" your body. Get yourself centered, clear your mind, and allow tones to come through you. The ancient mystery schools worked with sound in this manner, and it is a very powerful technique when done in a group. Many years down the road, but within this decade, you will amaze yourselves with what you will perceive as the results of your cooperative sounds or symphonies of consciousness playing themselves. When you tone together, you will be shown what you can do without even knowing you can do it. You will learn how to use and cultivate this kind of energy to make your own ankh. When you buy a child clay, the child at first doesn't know how to make many things, so you make little balls and spaghettis for the child so he or she can see the potential within the clay. Then the child, after playing with the clay for awhile, discovers his or her own sense of creativity with form.

The creative form of sound is shown to you first as a potential. You are led and orchestrated through the use of this sound. Eventually, you will discover on your own some of the things that sound can achieve. Then you will become more daring, and you will learn what sound can create. Energies are introduced this way to make certain there is not a misuse of them and that you don't overextend yourself or overdo out of enthusiasm.

You will go very far with your use of sound after working with it for awhile. It is like a powerful tool being given to an infant. Without proper awareness, you could do things and not realize the ramifications of what you are doing. Think about what sound does in stadiums and auditoriums. The cheering or booing of a crowd creates an ambience. When groups of you make sound together, you create an ambience for yourselves. You allow certain energies to play the instrument of your bodies. You let go of preconceived ideas and allow different melodies and energies to use your physical bodies as opportunities to represent themselves on the planet. In actuality, what you experience is the life force of energies that you allow to express through your own selves. You become channels. Just as our vehicle allows us to come into your reality through her body, you allow a vibration to come onto the planet in its full glory through your bodies and your joint cooperation. You birth something. You create an opportunity, and an energy takes advantage of that opportunity.

Emotion, because it brings feeling and connects you to feeling, allows you to recognize different states of consciousness. The logical mind does not allow you to recognize states of consciousness because it holds onto its own identity. It is locked into the boundary of ego and does not want to recognize other areas. Feeling, however, always acknowledges other areas because feeling discerns the difference. You can read the signs and the definitions by the energy that you call feeling. It is, in actuality, a vibration. Sound brings about states of emotional feeling. When you create harmonics of sound, it reminds your body of something. It reminds your body of light, of deep cosmic love, and of other worlds. Your body comes into joy and sometimes overwhelmingly into sadness. It seeks and accesses a frequency that it has been longing for, which the sound has reminded it of. As you allow sound to play your body, you discover a frequency that you have sought. This frequency is connected to the evolution of the helixes within your body. Sound is a vehicle or conduit to connect you to the higher chakras outside of your body because you do not have a way of accessing them logically. You must access all frequencies and chakra centers by feeling, and sound will connect you with feeling, which will allow you to understand the information.

If sound could be pictured, some of you would become entranced with watching it. There are realities where sound does picture itself. You feel the movement and language of sound when you wave your body or move your hands. You experience the richness of this form of communication and how multidimensional all things are by feeling sound express itself. It has its own language, and it has a form.

Sound carries a certain frequency, and the body recognizes the frequency. The body is keyed to respond to the acceptability of the frequency. The great master musicians such as Beethoven and Mozart were coded to bring in information of a stable nature, for they received the harmonics of sound at the time when there was great darkness over the planet. In order to keep a certain remembrance open in the minds of the human race, lower vibratory rates of sound were translated into the minds of these masters.

Sound is going to evolve. Now human beings can become the instruments for sound through toning. Human beings become the flute, the piano, the harp, the oboe, and the tuba. They allow energies to use their physical bodies to make a variety of sounds that they do not direct or attempt to control the range of. Spirit plays, and human beings simply observe the attendance of the symphony that they and all the others are performing. It is quite profound.

These harmonics can be utilized in incredible ways, for harmonics can evolve many things. One of the things that is important for utilizing these harmonics is to be very silent once the harmonics are complete. The harmonics alter something; they open the door. Certain combinations of sounds played through the human body unlock information and frequencies of intelligence. Being silent for a long period after the harmonics allows human beings to use their bodies as devices to receive and absorb the frequencies and to use the vehicle of breathing to take them into an ecstatic state.

When you tone with others, you have access to the group mind that you did not have prior to making the sound. It is a gigantic leap in consciousness. *The key word is harmony.* When the entire planet can create a harmonic of thought, the entire planet will change. That is what you are working for. You are going to broadcast a frequency, and that sound is going to travel. It is going to become a desperate aching and longing for the return to harmonics within the human race—a return to the power of the group mind and the simultaneous empowerment of the individual.

What you intend to do with sound is of the utmost importance. If you are not clear about your intentions, sound can have a way of enveloping upon itself and growing beyond its original capacity. It doubles and quadruples itself with its own impact. It is very important for you to have a clear intention of what you plan on doing with the sound. That is number one.

Number two is that sound stirs energy up. It creates a standing columnar wave, building frequency upon frequency. This energy can then be directed at or toward anything. You have heard about those who marched around the city of Jericho. They marched for days around Jericho and created a standing wave. The wave eventually built up so much energy that the city walls imploded.

Native dance, rattling, shaking, and moving in circles creates the energy of this wave. When you make sound in a circle, or in the circumference of the pillar of light, you create a column that is capable of doing many more things than you ever realized. It is capable of creating explosions and of destroying and creating many realities.

Among the war-oriented tribes, the warhoop was used by those who went into battle. The unified and intended invocation was to ask the nonphysical forces to accompany them. The warriors would use this kind of sound to combat their opponents by allowing energy to move through a portal and create a standing column. When you hear a sound like a warhoop, you remember uncomfortable ways that the sound has been utilized because it is very powerful. It makes others uncomfortable because it reminds them of the responsibility of sound. Some of you are petrified of sound; you are petrified of the sound of your own voice speaking out and stating with clarity what you prefer. You have cellular memory of what sound can achieve, and the impact or capability of what you can do with it is to some of you rather devastating. Sound can link you to places where your intellect cannot. Your intellect strives to categorize, but you cannot categorize sound; you must simply experience it.

Misuse happens through intent. You can discover the power of sound and then misuse it to manipulate others. What do you experience when you live in a city and hear sirens? Fear. That is a misuse of sound, and it is altering your frequencies. It is a very base way to do so. Those who make the sound know the results of it on the human psyche. It is jarring and disturbing and keeps you from placing your attention somewhere else. That frequency is like a lock; it is hypnotizing, and it captures your consciousness and your intelligence. It is as if your intelligence cannot focus any other place. It is almost like being in a prison, because the sound imprisons your awareness so that it becomes addicted to or locked into a vibratory rate and does not seek anything else. It becomes subdued. Think also of your televisions or the sound coming from other electrical devices.

It is always upsetting to look at the different forms of frequency control and to see how powerful allies such as sound are used to control you. It creates a great deal of anger, unrest, havoc, and excitement in many human beings when they hear about the undercover devices used to manipulate consciousness. We share these things with you for many reasons. The ultimate purpose is to bring you to greater self-empowerment. You must realize that you are not powerless in any situation and that your mind is the ultimate of your creativity. Your mind and your thoughts design your experience no matter what method of technology is being used.

Those who act in their own reality with impeccable guidance, commitment to harmony, and commitment to light align themselves with their dimensional counterparts who are doing the same. You make bridges of light and hold light-encoded filaments as pillars and open portals. Those who are rewarded with the understanding that they are called to use sound as part of their work and who recognize that call and respond to it will evolve at a rapid pace. Those of you evolving at this rate will be called one day to represent many people, to represent world gatherings of consciousness, and to change the available frequency with your sound.

NINETEEN

Igniting the Internal Flame

The planet is looking for a balance in the self. Since the self is a composite of all things, it is a harmonic that balances all of your extraterrestrial selves, multidimensional selves, and male and female selves.

You are incredibly whole beings, which you are beginning to realize. Allow yourself to blossom and come into this completeness. No one hinders you but yourself. If you allow this completion, there are vistas awaiting you that are beyond your imagination. You are discovering that you need your emotional body and that you need both your femininity and your masculinity. You need all that you have been gifted with in order to survive and understand what is unfolding upon the planet. Please realize the severity of the times that you are living in. As we spend time with each of you, you in turn will be tested and then taken to teach many others when the time comes.

Through feeling, you can discover much more, for you are seeking to resolve something and make something whole within yourself. To show yourself how unwhole you are, you have created a situation of tremendous separation that appears to be outside of yourself. It looks as if your drama has to do with a powerful man against a powerful woman. Which one is going to be the victim? Who is right and who is wrong? What is this internal drama actually saying? What is this outside mirror that images what is going on inside of you?

As you access multidimensionality, you must merge male and female. You will not stop at the separation or fight between men and women that has been going on for thousands of years. Who is creating the separation between men and women? It is the creator gods, who have set up this paradigm for you and instigated these frequencies from other points of view. The separation story has served them well because of the havoc it has created.

The male vibrations came into power in recent times some five thousand years ago. In order to slowly recognize who they were, they completely and totally disassociated themselves from anything that was formerly in power: the matriarchal movement and females. Females operate traditionally through the realms of intuition and feeling. Males have also been carriers of intuition and feeling a multitude of times, but in this recent separation they did not carry feelings with them. There was a huge schism, and the males and females on the planet came into great conflict. Why did this occur? It was a setup. It was set up by the creator gods who took over the planet and raided the reality—feeding, keeping themselves alive and functioning, and nourishing themselves off emotional turmoil.

This planet has been subjected to all kinds of plans and activities orchestrated to create greater and greater emotional turmoil. The more people involved in these activities, the more potential for emotional turmoil there has been. The creator gods instigated these activities and set you up to work against each other. In order to bust this paradigm, as you all are on assignment to do, you must change many of the separating structures that have been set up. Whatever the separation may be— between man and woman, black and white, or Oriental and Caucasian—you must change it.

You came onto the planet purposely to insert yourselves as members of the Family of Light in situations that are archetypal. As we have said, you are doing this so that you can understand the masses and transmute energy for them by being able to transmute it within yourself. Once you make a healing or joining, you take it on and heal not only yourself, you heal the species and the mass psyche. Remove yourselves from your personal drama and realize that it is all symbolic. See yourself as a female entity looking for identity, and notice how a male identity constantly seems to oppose you. You must discover how you can bring these identities together inside yourself. When this joining occurs inside you, it will automatically proceed outside you. As you have journeyed upon this planet, part of what you have come to heal is male dominion over the female. You don't need to take what you are doing personally or carry it as a personal burden as if it is just yours. It is not just yours; it is universal.

Each of you carries energies to resolve within your collective experience. As members of the Family of Light, you each have your reincarnational goodies—your "stuff"—in areas that most impersonate you and that you find to be stimulating. That is why you are all different. As members of the Family of Light, you need to branch out or fan out to get the hang of being human. You need to cover the full spectrum of experience so that you can comprehend from a cellular level how much needs to be transmuted, how deep the sense of powerlessness runs, and how lost the energy of the Goddess is from the consciousness of the species.

Remember, you are creatures who have been locked in development by frequency, and your task is to bring human beings to the place where they can be poised to consciously accelerate human evolution. When you are locked in evolution by frequency and DNA manipulation, there is only a certain kind of frequency that can broadcast. There is fighting with the self, and things seem to be more separated. As you become more complete, you do not separate things in such a way: you see that all things are part of the experience. Sometimes you become so lost in the experience of being human that you forget what you are here to do.

As members of the Family of Light, you have come here to transmute for the species. As soon as you get less attached to the dramas, you will not feel so caught up and victimized by them. You will understand that this is a collective of energy you are dealing with. So, collectively, if you can come to the realization inside yourselves, you can broadcast a new vibration for women and men to harmonize with.

Every time you feel as if you have made headway, you have. Do not discount the steps you have taken. You discredit yourself when you look at your behavior and judge yourself or others as bad. Look for what you get out of everything.

The conflict that is going on is actually between the male and female inside of you. You have not figured out how to merge your male and female parts, and there are millions of others with the same conflict. Be kind and generous to yourself. As you build cooperation between your male and female counterparts within yourselves, you will be able to find the cooperation to work with one another on the planet and the cooperation to work with the beings who come from space who are all yourselves.

You all need to become sovereign. As you change, you need to have a space around you within which you can operate without feeling obligated to someone else. At the same time, you cannot make demands on someone else without allowing them the same right. You are redefining in many ways the whole concept of relationship and cooperation. Relationship *is* cooperation. It is agreed cooperation of frequency, or frequency-modulation blending. Many of your old ways of relating are becoming very irritating because you are discovering a freedom frequency. Your assignment is to pull that freedom frequency onto the planet. Of course, you will pull it into your own life and family and relationships first. Ideally, you will learn how to be free while still being involved in an intricate number of relationships, relatings, and relayings of life.

Unfortunately, on this planet, relationships connote ownership. When a man and woman get married, the woman's father traditionally has the role of giving her away. In other words, a male figure must hand her over. There is an incredible expectancy within relationships about another's behavior. Get clear about what your idea of relationship is, and this will facilitate things in the long run. Just as there is no ownership with parenthood, there is no ownership in a relationship. You relate to one another as you relate energies back and forth. Ideally, there is communication with all of this relaying and relating. The male vibrations give their power away just as much as the females. They give it away to a government that says, "Here, go jeopardize your life. Go take a stand and shoot for us. If your body gets chopped up, we will take care of you in a hospital and give you a bit of money. What the heck; go for it," and the males just obey. The chain of obeying and giving the power of the individual away is then complete.

You are opening your feeling centers. Men tend to have greater blocks in their feeling centers than women do. Energy in the male has been stuck, because it has moved from the first chakra to the second chakra and stopped. The feeling center in the male vibration has not been activated. This is part of the experiment that has gone on for the last four or five thousand years. The female energy, which feels and brings life onto the planet and represents creativity, moved into a submissive state in order for the male vibration to have its opportunity, without feeling, to run the world.

We want you to get the big picture. We are looking at movements of consciousness. The female, who carried the magic and the intuitive, agreed to give these up—female meaning not just female physical beings but *consciousnesses* who were female. Many of the native cultures that lived with Earth and knew about life were very feminine. Remember, the female literally brings life onto the planet, for life comes out of the female body. The female therefore carries feelings, because you can't bring life onto the planet and not feel—unless you participate in the patriarchal movement that creates drugs to numb you from feeling. When you can't feel life, you don't value life. When you feel life and participate in the creation and deliverance of life, you value life much more because you know about it.

The patriarchal movement over the last five thousand years

has removed itself from the birthing process so that it could carry out its experimentations involving war and the continual annihilation of people. The energy was purposely blocked in the male. As we mentioned, the male energy is very stuck. We are not pointing fingers. However, we are saying, in general, that the energy of the male species on the planet is very stuck in the second chakra or within the penis. Females, you are stuck in your throats because you agreed four or five thousand years ago to be silent about the magic and intuition of what you represented and knew as one part of the twin flame. The twin flame is the male and female existing in one body, whether you are physically male or female.

The patriarchal society has been run by the male aspect of the self, which you all have been. You have all experimented with consciousness and taught yourselves about what works best, preparing for this time when the flames will be lit together in your body. At this time, the twin flame is not sought as a partner outside of the self but is understood to be the integration of the male and female selves and the ripeness of all that self has done. After you have integrated the male and female within yourself and activated your own twin flame, then, when you seek a partner, you will seek someone complete, not someone to fill the need that you have not acknowledged or that you have not filled for yourself.

During these times of change, women are going to need to open their throats and give themselves permission to speak out. Now is the time. And men, your challenge in understanding women and other men is to feel, and to let feeling enter your expression of sexuality in your relationships. Many men now are having a very difficult time with women. Women are driving men crazy. It is true.

What we are suggesting for the male vibration—and also for the female who operates in the male aspect of herself—is that you move into feeling in your sharing of sexuality. Move into the emotionality of things, rather than just the sexuality and stimulation of the body. There is an emotional stimulation that needs

emotional commitment and emotional trust. Electromagnetically, this emotional stimulation will open a frequency within you. This frequency that sexuality represents is a reminder
of your godhood.

The male shut down his feeling center in order to experience
stewardship upon this planet. He was able to carry on war and
to kill and dominate the planet because he had shut down his
feeling center. The female agreed to have her speaking center
shut down so that the male would have the opportunity to experience being in charge of this system.

All of this is now coming to a point of stabilization or
equalization. The female began to open her throat about thirty
years ago, making the opportunity to speak fashionable. The
problem is that many females ended up shutting down their
feeling centers as they opened their speech centers. They began
to become very much like males. A balance is needed. Now the
female is finding the need to awaken the feminine principle inside herself. She is in a female body and has mastered the use of
the male vibration within herself. She has gone out into the
world, and she feels powerful. She can walk the streets without
a veil on her face, and she can decide whether she wants to be
married. She is her own property. She is responsible in this
country for her own decisions. She is beginning to soften and to
awaken the portion of herself that nurtures her and brings her
life. As she makes herself whole with her male and her female
portions and allows herself to experience the evolved DNA, she
broadcasts this frequency. This frequency will become very
prevalent upon the planet.

It is inevitable that men will open their feeling centers. That
is the next step men must go through to establish a balance with
the female. This will happen very quickly for men. It will not be
a thirty-year process because men at this time are moving as a
populace into confusion. Men are realizing that they don't like
what is occurring, and they are questioning authority.

At some point, the frequencies will become predominant.
Then, for example, a person may be experimenting on an animal

in a laboratory when their feeling center is suddenly and radically opened. The person feels the pain that the animal is feeling, and what they have been doing becomes abhorrent. They turn around and walk away from the laboratory and never go back because they are so shaken. This is what is coming for the male vibration.

We have said that the male vibration will transform in a very short period of time. We will not tell you why or how because some of you will consider it to be entirely too ominous. However, we will say that, as the waves continue to come, there will be a unilateral rising of consciousness within the population. At a certain point, when men are in the deepest struggle of mastering feeling, the feeling center will be activated. This will either occur gently, or it will be blown wide open.

Women at the same time will be hit, infused, and enveloped with the opening of the heart chakra so that they can have compassion while they watch their men feel. We are speaking of mass events that will trigger people through waves of light.

Female energy, that which feels and connects life to life, is being awakened in everyone. Women must redefine their ideas of femaleness and strength. They must find what it is to be strong as females, just as men must discover what it is to be vulnerable as males. What is the endearing aspect of the male when he is vulnerable? What is the endearing aspect of the female when she is in self-empowerment—when she is a feminine version of empowerment and not a masculine version?

Women have had a hard shell around their energy fields; they have been protecting themselves. Now they are going to develop true emotional strength. That hard outer shell will diffuse, and the light body will radiate from the heart. The goddesses and the gods are agreeing and working with this energy. It is so decreed that this is how the drama will unfold.

The old stories have been buried and covered that recount the magic of the female, the creator, the one able to bring birth, the one holding the mystery of blood—the life force—and the one able to put that life force back into Earth. Where are the stories of the Goddess—she who loves and feels and nurtures? The male species used to have Goddess energy inside, too, and felt the need for the Goddess.

In order to better control the planet during the last several thousand years, all of the myths have been given to you by extraterrestrials. They have seeded all of your religious institutions. We have said you are an experiment. At times, the experiment has been uplifting and loving, but in recent times it has moved into incredible decay. You, as members of the Family of Light, have come to raid this planet and pull light back onto it so that the nonsense of separation and war never need be believed again. Man and woman are meant to complement each other, not oppose each other.

Remember, feeling is emotion. Emotion is the key to getting off this planet; it is the key to figuring out the multidimensional self, healing it, and becoming one. It is also the key to lovingly activating Earth as a Living Library, returning a valuable area of existence from extinction. With men and patriarchal society in charge of this planet for the last several thousand years, and women taking a position underground—not even in the back seat—separation has been the theme and emotion has been pushed aside, given a bad name, and frowned upon. You have been automatons, performing roles that were given to you to keep you separated.

You do not have a pantheon of powerful female creator images. You have nothing on which to pattern a positive image of the empowered feminine. So men are striving to be male and women are striving to be empowered through a male vibration because you do not have a clear vision of the empowered female. *You must create it.* Begin to recognize the wealth of energy in the female version of self, which is intuition, receptivity, creativity, compassion, and nourishment. You are discovering that there is a wealth of identity in an essence that has been discredited for a long time. If you are female, of course, you are a living form of that essence. Men must discover their form of the

Goddess within themselves where the Goddess meets the god in them.

By the same token, the view of the masculine is distorted. You do not have an example of an empowered, *feeling* male. Society has deemed feeling males "soft" and lacking in masculinity. Men are beginning to look at their emotions and say, "Hey, I *feel* this," and know that they are still men. So men and women are both creating role models for empowered, integrated versions of masculine and feminine. These models are coming, and they are coming quickly. The time for separation is finished.

As we mentioned, it is not *outside* yourself that you are looking for a twin flame partner. You are looking for the integration of the female and male essence within yourself. They make one whole. Whole people are looking to connect with other whole people in relationships that are based on trust, desire, and choice. The relationships are not based on "I need you in my life to complete me and validate me." You become complete in yourself and operate with someone else who is complete in themself and offers a whole new territory to explore.

When you marry that twin flame inside yourself, you are recognizing the intuitive, Goddess, life-bringing, sensitive portion of yourself as well as the portion of yourself that is powerful, rational, and intellectual. One that is very much of the Earth plane and the other is very much of the spiritual plane. When you merge these energies together in yourself, it will be imperative that you find someone who has the same qualities. You will not fit with someone who is not integrated and whole.

You will automatically draw whole people to yourself, and it will be effortless. You will be able to plug into one another out of desire and recognition, not out of need. You will achieve something that you never recognized as a possibility in any relationship before, and you will give relationship a very new personality, a new boundary, and a new definition. You will become your own role models for this new type of relationship. Many of you will find that the marriage institution is meaningless. It will not fit and house what you know or how you want to live.

As all of you are on the path of integrating the polarities within yourselves, difficult issues are going to come up over and over again. Welcome the difficult times, for they can be your greatest teacher. Stay focused on your own growth, your own path, and your own self, and not on what others are doing. Call on your own internal masculine and feminine and set up a dialogue between them so they can begin to work in partnership and harmony. Give yourself a lot of love and encouragement. Make an appointment with yourself and say, "I love you, self. You are a wonderful self. You are A-Number-One, the best self."

When you give yourself the dignity of your own love, as if you were royalty receiving the accolades of the people, everything changes. Strength and integration become yours because you believe in and love who you are. When you believe in and love yourself, everything starts to go your way. The most difficult thing for most of you is making the commitment to believe you deserve love. No one else has to love you. You are not here to go around gathering love from other people to convince yourself that you are worth it.

You are here to master a very difficult task in a system that is dark and gives very little input, stimulation, or information about the true story. You are here to do the impossible. By committing to love yourself and making this commitment the number-one step from which you operate every day, everything falls into place. You become whole and complete. Then you are ready for a bonded relationship with another who is complete, and that relationship can take you into unexplored realms.

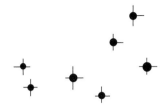

TWENTY

Sexuality—A Bridge to Higher Levels of Consciousness

When the library of yourselves was torn from the shelves and scattered, and the DNA was split so that there were only two strands left with very little data and very little memory, sexuality was left intact in the physical body. It was left as a form of reproduction, of course—as a form for the species to stay in touch with its own essence and bring itself into life. Very deep inside the mechanism of sexuality is a frequency that can be attained that has been sought after and misunderstood by many people. It is called orgasm.

The orgasm has been distorted from its original purpose. Your body has forgotten the cosmic orgasm of which it is capable because society has taught you for thousands and thousands of years that sexuality is bad. You have been taught this in order for you to be controlled and to keep you from seeking the freedom available through sexuality. Sexuality connects you with a frequency of ecstasy, which connects you back to your divine source and to information.

Sexuality has been given a bad name upon this planet, and that bad name is stored in your cellular memory. This is not just from this lifetime; it is from thousands of years of misappropriation and misuse. It is necessary for you to clear the negativity surrounding sexuality from this lifetime, as well as to experience and examine how you utilize sexual energy and sexual expression in your multidimensional selves.

The sexual parts of the body are avenues to pleasure that create frequencies that heal and stimulate the body and potentially lead it to its higher spiritual self. Sexuality is so misunderstood on this planet that, when it is exchanged between two persons, very seldom is there an intent to connect spirituality with it. Sexuality invokes a spirituality that is free and that looks at itself as a creator. However, very seldom is sexuality used as a bridge to take you to higher levels of consciousness.

We have spoken with a number of individuals who have been utilizing light. Since finding the proper partner in a monogamous situation, they have been able to achieve very high states of being. Monogamy tends to work for most of you very well because of where you are vibrationally. When you have many partners, you tend to be less than honest and to hide who you are: you share a little here, there, and everywhere in scattering your seed. It is best to be with one person, but this does not mean the same person forever. Be loyal, be open, and be sharing with the person you are working with, and go as far as you can with them. If it happens to be your whole life, wonderful. If it doesn't, then when you come to a place where you are no longer communicating and serving one another, and you feel the relationship is not going to be able to make a leap, terminate the relationship and find another person who works with your vibration.

When you work one-on-one intimately, you develop trust. Most of you have difficulty trusting yourselves because you don't have a role model for trust. You can learn about trust in a relationship because a relationship acts as a mirror for you, showing you what you cannot see from your own viewpoint. It shows you yourself outside of yourself when you have open communication within sexuality and deep intimacy, and when you are not using sexuality as a distraction for getting close. Many of you have used sexuality as a distraction and a way to avoid intimacy rather than to develop it. You begin to get energy and to look into one another's eyes and to feel all hot and excited. Then, instead of exploring each other intimately and spiritually, you shut down your feeling centers, put on your armor, and have shallow, genital sex because it is too frightening and too intense to go the deeper route of full body and full spiritual connection. Sometimes hot sex feels great and is wonderful. We are simply saying that there is more. There is much more, and no one is keeping it from you except yourselves and the beliefs and fear you have of letting down your boundaries and walls.

Many of the fears you have are based on what you have created for yourselves and what you have done to others in your sexual life. Your sexual history affects every other portion of your soul, so all of your soul's issues are broadcast loud and clear throughout your body. You don't want to look at this sometimes because it is too painful, and you judge it because you think it is bad. Stop judging, and get neutral about what you have done—no matter what you discover, no matter how heinous it seems, no matter how difficult it seems, and no matter how much violation it involves. Understand that your purpose has been to gather data and to understand your selves.

Sexuality is a frequency. It represents what was not taken away from you even though your history, your memories, and your identity were removed and scattered. The way you were left intact with the ability to discover who you were was through the sexual experience. Of course, you were never taught this. We are going to do some church bashing here. So sorry for anyone who is a member of the churches. The churches came about as organizations—businesses to control religion and spiritual development and to create jobs, to create a hierarchy, and to create a club. Very few churches came about with the idea of bringing information to people. You don't usually think of religion as something that keeps you informed, do you? Any religion that brings information is a religion operating on the vibration of truth.

Spiritual realms are places of existence that the human body is locked away from. Because sexuality was an opportunity for human beings to regain their memory, or to connect with their spiritual selves and spiritual creator, or to find an avenue to the spiritual realm that you are sealed off from, the churches came about and promoted sexuality for procreation. They taught you that the only reason you had sexuality was to produce little humans.

Sexuality was promoted as something very bad. Women were told that sexuality was something they had to undergo to serve men and that they had no control over the birthing process. Women believed this; hence, to this day, you believe in general that you have no control over that portion of your body. You must realize that only you decide whether you are going to birth a child or not. This is not such a complicated thing as you have been told. Decision and intention are what bring the experience to your being. You can control whether you have a baby or not. If woman had had this ability for the last several thousand years, and if she had been able to explore her sexual self without fear of having a child, perhaps men and women would have discovered that they were much freer than they had been told they were.

The discovery of the highest frequency of sexuality arises from the love experience. It has nothing to do with relationships being either homosexual or heterosexual. It has to do with two human beings bringing pleasure to one another in a way that opens frequencies of consciousness. You have bought many ideas about what is proper and what is improper within sexual expression.

Love is the essence that is to be created in all relationships. If you love and honor someone, it doesn't matter what your composition of density is. What matters is the love vibration and how you explore this love, which ideally is gifted and coupled with the integration of the male and the female counterparts that make the twin flame.

Ideally, sexuality is explored through feelings. The third and fourth chakras connect you to the emotional and compassionate selves, which connect you to the spiritual self. The spiritual self is the part of yourself that is multidimensional—through which you exist in many forms simultaneously. It is your assignment and agreement and task to be aware of all these realities in the identity that you are. When you are aware, you can tune into the different frequencies, remember who you are, and change the vibratory rate of this universe.

We love to talk about sexuality because it is so mysterious upon this planet. Certain mystery schools have held some of the knowledge about the potential uses of sexuality in secrecy. You are electromagnetic creatures, and when you come together physically with another human creature, you bond your electromagnetic frequencies together. When your frequencies are attuned and joined by a love frequency, incredible things can occur.

Thousands of years ago, when society had more of a matriarchal view in certain areas of the planet, Goddess energy was coming through and working with certain individuals. The female understood her power, her intuition, her feeling center, her connection, and her desire to create life. She also understood that *she never had to conceive a child if it was not her intention to do so.*

In order for the patriarchal society to come full circle and prepare Earth for this shift in consciousness, female energy needed to take a back seat. So female power, energy, and understanding of sexuality were suppressed. In modern times—the past two thousand years—it came to be upon the planet that women believed they had no control over when they could have children, that sexuality was deemed bad and disgusting, and that sex was taught to be performed only within the rights of marriages and so on. All of this was a marketing program.

Some of the present-day marketing programs to create an even greater fear of sexuality and its expression are the new diseases: AIDS, herpes, and all the other things. You read about these things in your newspapers and become frightened of your own expression, frightened of your own intuition, and frightened of your own joy. Do you understand?

Before DNA was rearranged, the way many people reached

the higher realms and were able to climb the ladders of themselves and reach into off-planet frequencies was by electromagnetically bonding through love. They created a rocketship-like
experience to propel them out into other systems of reality. This
has been one of the best-kept secrets upon the planet.

Many we have spoken to have had absolutely profound experiences with their sexuality. We would like to point out again
that we are not making distinctions or judgments about who
you happen to bond with in a relationship, and we suggest that
you give up that judgment as well. It is old programming. It
does not matter whether you bond with a member of the opposite sex or a member of your own sex. We are talking about
two humans coming together by physically joining themselves
in whatever ways are appropriate for them to join and create
love, because they are sharing love. When integrity and love are
missing from a joining of human bodies, that is when human
beings do not think well of their experience. This can create all
kinds of damaging results within the physical body.

You were left with the frequency of the orgasmic experience
in sexuality so that you could remember your higher identity.
When this energy or history of yourself is revealed and you
discover who you are, you will unite many bodies of your
personal multidimensional identity in your physical form. To
receive the full impact of the gridwork of your identity, let the
twelve helixes fit in your body and allow the light-encoded
filaments to rearrange themselves. This process has to do with
the mental body, which is of course connected to the physical
body. The emotional body, which is connected to the spiritual
body, is the body that everybody wants to skip. You say, "I want
to evolve. I want a rapid acceleration, but I do not want to go
through the feeling center to do it."

You are connected to your multidimensional selves through
your feelings, and it is in your feelings that you primarily get
stuck. Accept that your "stuff" comes up for a reason. Many of
you would like to bury your "stuff" and throw it out in the trash
as if it is something ugly and not who you are. This "stuff" is the

shadow portion of your identity that you don't like to deal with or accept.

We understand that sometimes, when something comes up, you label it and say, "I hate this part of myself. I want to just finish it and sweep it under the rug and forget it. I'm finished with this stuff." Guess what. Your "stuff"—your issues—are the treasures of your life. They are how you learn.

You have agreed to mutate, to pull light into your body, and to birth the Family of Light on this planet. Since light is information, you must deal with all of the things you have hidden from yourself. Sexuality is the primary issue because it is the secret self—the self you hide from. Society has said to you, "This is good. This is bad. You are to do this. You are not to do this." Who gave you these laws? Who gave you any of your laws to begin with?

You have been stuck because you can't read the symbols of the language you are speaking to yourselves. So you dwell upon it. Many of you love your stories because they get you attention. If you didn't have a story, who would talk to you? Observe your body and see what it is teaching the self. Ideally, you will heal the sore and create a place of greater comfort and joy as you learn to dwell more completely in your physical body and have a new identity of your sexuality.

Sexuality is a key. It is a doorway to the higher realms of consciousness. As you redefine yourselves, and the light-encoded filaments give you a new definition of yourselves, you are going to change who you are sexually as well. Sexuality must come up for all of you, and, we will say from experience, it is the area that you are most frightened of at this time. We guarantee there will be more frightening areas later.

If you are stuck on the idea of love and cannot comprehend what is going on with it, your difficulty is that you are looking for love outside yourself. You are looking for somebody else to put meaning in your life and validate you. If you do not have that person, you become angry or feel you are worthless. This is a pattern you grew up with, which your parents and your society showed you. We have said over and over again that the most important thing you can do is love yourself and honor Earth. But you keep forgetting this and looking for the next relationship to make you whole or complete. You feel that without a relationship you are perhaps less than an acceptable citizen. Then you feel lonely. You must learn how to be alone. Loneliness is simply a state of mind. You are never, never alone. You have multitudes of entities around you. If you would stop feeling sorry for yourselves, you would find that there is so much data constantly being blasted at you that you may want to be alone so you can have a good time receiving the contact.

When you love yourself and stop getting convoluted about the need to have someone else love you, you are able to accept what someone offers. It is imperative that you value yourself so that you do not settle for a love disguised. If you decide to go for a partner or to vibrate with someone, and you do not receive what you want, do not whine or nag or pout about the person to make them change according to your needs. If you set a value for yourself and do not create it, then simply change your reality and continue onward alone until you meet someone who reflects your value. All the while, vibrate in the love of the self, honor the self, and understand that the journey here is about *self-discovery* in relationship to others. It is not just about husbands or wives. The journey here is about honoring your physical body and the uniqueness of the self as you touch the lives of many. Always allow yourself to work with the self and let the self evolve.

You are all afraid of being intimate with yourselves—of being alone with the self. Once you develop an intimacy, a silence, a self-love, and a containment of your energy, then you will want to make that aspect of intimacy your standard for intimacy with someone else.

Sexuality can be very confusing at this time because you are raising and studying your frequencies. When you join bodies, even when you hug one another, you exchange frequency. When you have a sexual experience, there is a hormonal release inside the body. The hormones awaken certain energies inside the cells, and there is a transference of one person's essence onto the other person. That is why when you have had sexual experiences with someone you sometimes cannot get their energy off you. Even though you don't want to be with the person, the sexual experience stays with you because you have had an electromagnetic exchange.

You are going through this frequency modulation and learning how to raise your frequency to a place of consistent information, self-love, and self-intimacy. Therefore, it can seem very confusing and sometimes frightening to take this vulnerable thing you are learning about yourself and layer up and merge with another. The more you become aware, the more you take charge of how you use your body, where you plug it in, where you sit it down, and certainly who you mix it with sexually.

If expressing yourself sexually now encouraged your greatest growth, you would automatically create that experience for yourself because you would be ready for it. Understand that, during the process of evolving the self, very often a period of dormancy in sexual activity occurs. Within the sexual frequency, you exchange with one another. So if you are bonding yourself and chemically exchanging with a person who is not of your likeness, you are taking on their garbage because you are exchanging energy quite intimately.

Sometimes you will be led away from that kind of exchange. You may think, "Oh, my goodness, what is happening? Am I turning old? Am I drying up? What is going on?" That is not the case. You can learn to use the energy that would stimulate you sexually without giving it over to another person. Instead of getting chaotic and crazy, you may explore that energy by practicing the art of masturbation, knowing that it is perfectly legitimate and fine to do it. Or, you may want to simply observe that you feel a sexual arousal and decide what you are going to do with it. You may say, "Well, I'm not going to act on this now. Let's see where this energy goes." Take the energy, let it rise through your body, and use it in other areas.

You will get to a point when you must adore, sustain, and love yourself as if you are holding yourself like a newborn babe in your own arms, knowing you will do the best for yourself. Many of you distract yourselves. Find the place of serenity and silence in which you can find answers. You cannot find answers by dialing the telephone all day long and asking everyone else for them. If you attempt to, you are demonstrating that you are looking outside of yourself. When you learn how to turn within to find answers, the self will speak. Usually you cannot hear because you are locked in behavioral patterns that you know you have to change but that you don't want to change because you don't know who you will be.

In all honesty, you are afraid of yourselves. This is a very common thing. You are afraid you will not be complete, and you want to be complete very much. So you say, "I am complete. I am sovereign. I need someone else. I am attracted to someone. Oh, no, I cannot look. I am too frightened of that. I don't need anyone. I do need someone." You go back and forth. Learn to still your mind. Learn to become completely in charge of your energy. What does that mean? It means that wherever you are, you observe yourself—how your body is positioned, how you are using your hands, whether you are repeating yourself over and over again, whether you are speaking or silent. Learn to watch yourself with no judgment. Learn to watch and self-correct by determining how you would like to be versus how you are. Learn to quiet your mind.

Frequency is carried from you to another person particularly if there is a love bonding. A love bonding does not mean that you are going to cleave to one another forever. It simply means that you are in a relationship for however long you deem that relationship appropriate in that you honor one another and exchange energies and let the energies flow as if through open circuitry. When you do not love another and you are not bonded, there is no exchange; the circuitry does not open. It does not mean that you cannot have good sex; it simply means that the circuitry is not open.

As this electrical current is raised higher and higher, there are greater heights of orgasmic experience that the human body can receive because the nervous system is able to handle the higher ecstatic frequencies. The nervous system will determine how you express yourself and how you feel. If you have a poorly evolved nervous system, your sexual experience will be very limited because the nervous system conducts the electrical current. The orgasmic experience brings about a healing and realignment of the physical body.

Eventually, you will not be able to get close to or be with someone who is not operating at the same voltage you are. You simply will not fit. It would be like putting a size nine foot into a size two shoe. It won't work or be comfortable. You won't fit because you won't be able to merge vibrationally.

You will eventually understand the importance of vibrational nourishment as you begin to link sexually. Linking sexually is only one way of merging with people who are moving at the same or a compatible voltage rate. Your reality is very interesting to us because you have so many clues in your waking world. When you go to a foreign country, your electrical appliances do not plug in. They don't fit, so you need an adapter. It would be stressful if you had to continuously adapt to a vibration when you were involved intimately in a sexual relationship. It would be too much effort. You would spend all your energy creating the adaptive mechanisms. Then you would be in denial and not give yourself permission to go further because you would lower the ceiling.

The sixties marked the opening of sexual exploration. In an instant, the paradigm shifted. Much of the energy that was on the planet at that time, coupled with the experimental ingestion of different mind-altering substances, immediately made a new paradigm and split you from previous generations. The boundaries were instantly changed. You were split from a generation that believed in war and did not feel—a generation whose sexual expression was done in the dark, perhaps with many clothes on. You broke the paradigm wide open in many ways, and you set new trends and created new ways of being. It was wonderful. "Oh, goodness, free sex and love and bodies showing!" you said.

Now it is time for a whole new revolution through which you will become vibrationally hooked to a person. There will be no more distractions of sexuality and no more pretending that you are without hang-ups—that you are sexually liberated because you can be in this position and that position and say this and do that. That is simply body aerobics in the area of sexuality. We want you to get into the aerobics and contortions of the soul—the vibration. The depth of two people coming together and linking in this capacity is what you all crave. If you are frightened of it, it is because you don't have a framework or role model for it. You must design one. You must trust that somehow the energy in the design of the cosmic blueprint will instantly bring about a new movement based on the desire for this next step of understanding yourselves.

You will remember with great clarity your expressions of sexuality in your different manipulations through reality—when you have been both men and women and explored sexuality in every aspect. It takes courage to do this. If there is one area in which you really judge yourselves, and in which the planet does great judging, it is sex. You have had some definite ideas about what is sexually proper and improper. So, many of you may be shocked to remember what you have done with your sexuality.

Understand that, on this planet, sexuality has always been the body's link to its higher frequency. Even though much of the data was scattered and disassembled in the body, this potential to create life remained for you to completely understand who you are at the base of your being and at the core of who you are. Sexual vibration has been your link with your cosmic identity, but this whole concept has been completely misunderstood and lost. We are simply saying that there is a bigger story and that it is much more exciting than anyone has dared to believe.

There were those who did not want you to be in tune with these frequencies because the sexual frequencies could have taken you to areas of liberation where you would have begun to figure things out. Sexuality was left as a frequency for you to ride through the nervous system and connect with the higher mind by going out of your body. If you had been told that this was the route out, who could have controlled or manipulated you?

The population must clear the negative connotations and judgments that have colored your sexual experience for eons. You must make peace with sex in order to integrate the frequencies and identity. Things have been manipulated and given a boundary of limitation so that the truth of sexuality has been kept from you. You have been told that you can procreate with it and have orgasms, but you have not been told that you can open frequencies with it. You can come into contact and use it as a method of remembering who you are and altering the vibrational frequency of your body.

In the next few years, your expression of sexuality will have a whole new dimension. You will evolve and grow, provided that you have a partner who is willing to take the same route and to be that open. But if you are with someone who wants to play the avoidance game or the game of denial, you will not get there.

TWENTY-ONE

Your Commitment to Evolve in 3-D

From our point of view, you all have knowledge, and you just need to activate the memory that is stored inside your being. We've noticed that some of you, from your location of experience, are out there moaning and groaning, saying, "We need help and assistance now and again." So let us suggest to you an avenue that you can definitely walk down—a formula that works.

The formula is quite simple. It is for you, in the moment and every day, to consistently set out with clarity what you wish to experience. Perhaps what you want falls into a category of impossibility according to someone else's boundary or someone else's limitation. With a sense of deserving and graciousness, discover inside yourself what will bring you happiness. What makes you feel light and connected and alive? What do you desire that will bring peace on the planet as you occupy your own being?

Whatever those things are, begin to want them. Call them to yourself by saying, "It is my intention that I experience a harmonious lifestyle. It is my intention to experience health and energy that lead me to creative adventures. It is my intention that I be well provided for, that shelter and food and all of the things I need to experience life be given to me in great abundance, and that I pass this great abundance on and share it with others." These are not ideas you have been trained to think of.

Two or three times a day, devote a small portion of your time to getting clear about what you want. Every day open the energy centers in your body and above your body by calling the frequency of light. We call this the pillar of light. Picture a beam of light coming into your twelve chakra centers, seven inside your body and five outside your body. These chakras are information centers or vortexes that, once activated, begin to spin. When they spin, they create a movement inside your body that activates the light-encoded filaments to work together, rebundle, and form the twelve evolving helixes in the body.

It is very important for everyone who wishes to be in complete balance with their physical being to practice, on a regular basis, some kind of deep-breathing program. This is a program in which breath is very important and oxygenation is practiced so that oxygen is brought into the body.

Another activity we recommend for those of you who wish to move into a vast acceleration of energy is spinning. Move from left to right, spinning around and focusing your vision on your thumb, counting and spinning. We recommend that you spin thirty-three times at least once a day. You may build up to the thirty-three spins very slowly. If you are able to work up to thirty-three spins, three times a day, so that you are spinning ninety-nine times, well, we will see how long you stay on the planet—or at least in this dimension. When you complete spinning, however many times you spin, bring your palms together at chest level. Press them together, keeping your eyes open, and balance yourself with your feet a shoulder's width apart so that you feel anchored and still feel the spinning at the same time. This tremendously accelerates the spinning of the chakra systems inside your body, which tremendously accelerates the rate at which you can interpret and receive data.

So, the methods to use are intention, breathing, using the pillar of light, and spinning. We will add a postscript to thse. As you are electronic beings who are altering your frequency at a very fast rate, we would recommend that you drink a tremendous amount of water: fresh water, purified water, or spring water. Water acts as a conduit or conductor. It keeps your system open and flowing.

There are many other things you can do. Learn to have altered-state experiences and not feel out of control. Cultivate them and go into them to gather information, change probabilities, move onto the corridor of time, and alter your own lives. Then come out of them with complete and total use of your will with respect to how you use these altered states. When you learn to do this, the acceleration will be absolutely phenomenal. When there are many consciousnesses on the planet registering that kind of ability, the whole network that organizes and monitors human consciousness alters itself. More energy is able to come onto the planet because there are those who can accommodate it.

Everyone can learn to accommodate and honor this energy, because it must be housed. It is like an oil well. What good do oil wells do if they are untapped and shooting off here, there, and everywhere? Very little; they just create a mess. However, when you take energy gifts from Earth such as oil wells or sources of natural gas or waterfalls and you combine them with your will, you put together a purpose or way of directing the energy. Then a wealth occurs for those of you who direct these natural resources. The most essential aspect of this entire process of directing and housing energies is to value Earth and her experience first and foremost. You are being given an incredible natural resource at this time, and you must tap it and direct it. Then you will all become very wealthy individuals in the realms of accessibility and mastery.

Many of you want to reach the higher realms and stay there, forgetting that your task is here on Earth. You must learn to stay grounded. The necessity of being grounded is something many of you do not understand. You will soon find out that if you move into greater and greater acceleration and you do not have grounds—things to connect you and pull the worlds into one— you may have difficulty with your nervous systems. When frequency changes and more light comes into the body, the typical vehicle begins to receive much more data. Sometimes you get very bored living in your world, and you just want to come into data receptivity and forget about what you consider the mundane world. If you are not grounded, you will not have a way of allowing that information to enter your reality and be put to use. It could simply overload your system, or you could not be able to translate what you are getting and stay calm.

You need to balance many worlds at once. How do you do this? By intention, by practice, and by decree. Grounding allows worlds to merge and allows you to access many worlds. It allows you to feel surges of energy and then to direct these surges of energy where and when you need them—to become superhuman.

A good way to ground yourself is to go outside and sit on the ground. So go outside and be in nature. Stand or sit next to a tree for awhile. Put your chair in the sun and read a book with the sun shining on you. Or go swimming, or put your feet in water. These are the elements. They make up Earth, so you can feel them.

As you evolve and your entire species moves to merge dimensions, your nervous systems must be able to translate all of this information that will change how you define your world. This is coming. In the last year, the information that you may have known for years has become much more public. Many more people who have not been interested in extraterrestrials or personal development have become either interested or at least aware of these things. They are aware that there is a growing movement and that something is changing all over the world, not just in the United States.

There is a conflict of energies at this time, which you could call either a skirmish or a grand battle. The battle is going to become grander still because it is a battle over whose frequency will prevail on this planet and who will own, manipulate, and train your frequency. Who are you, as a frequency in disguise as a human, and what specifically is your job in this time?

It is essential to know who you are and what you are doing when you are doing it. As you become interdimensional and multidimensional, and as the frequencies alter and the energies accelerate, your body goes through a drastic rapid change that the nervous system, the conveyer of information, must handle.

You must learn to handle many realities at once, to realize that you are doing this, and to have a place—Earth—to translate information into. You would not be here if it wasn't important for you to ground information and energy into Earth. So whenever you find yourself electrified or energized, realize that you are in an altered state. Realize also how many versions of altered states there are and that you must instruct yourself to become a conduit, like a big pipeline. When you know you are in an altered state and are being given information, healing energy, exaltation, or upliftment, act as a pipeline. Funnel the energy through yourself, and acknowledge and recognize that you are in a multidimensional expression. Register this, but do not analyze it. Just let the energy filter through you into Earth, and it will make more sense later on.

You can discover your emotional body by making a decree that you believe emotions can be trusted. Decree that you believe emotions are good, that they are safe, that they can take you somewhere, that they are beneficial, and that they are not just in the way or misunderstood. Any time emotions are released in you, look to see what they do for you. When you have a fight with your child and your child screams at you and then afterwards you feel bad and cry, look at your emotion. What is the emotion doing for you? Whenever you are in emotion, you are accessing information from many realities. Find that frequency and hold it.

It is somewhat of a universal belief that emotions are uncontrollable. They are not. You can control emotion, and you do not have to go out of control. Emotion can become a frequency inside of you through which you feel to the depth and core of your being. Yet, someone may look at you and not have any idea that anything is going on with you. This does not mean you are blocking; it simply means you have set up a way to feel an emotion and not feel bad about it or good about it but just recognize you are feeling it. See what you can do with an emotion. Where does it take you? What is the next step? Disengage from the event that brought about the emotion. That will help some of you.

Bodywork serves to bring about a release. You have used the tissue and muscle of your body as armor to cover up your skeleton. This tissue has compacted and buried itself and kept what is in the skeletal form from rising to the surface. You want to access information that is within bone, for bone is where the story is held, while the blocks are held in tissue. You must go through all of these layers to get to the truth inside your body.

Your blueprint, or what you came onto this planet to achieve, begins to get excited when you get close. This is just like the game you played when you were a child; you would hide something, and when someone got close, you would say, "warmer." Your body gets excited as your blueprint begins to take over and you move out of your logical mind and into experience. That is because you are aligning yourself with your purpose. Your body, not your mind, takes in the information. If you allow your emotions to have a free reign, you will have a much more satisfying experience than if you judge your emotions, do not understand what you are going through, and attempt to control them.

You need your emotions. We cannot emphasize that enough. Some of you pride yourselves on the fact that you don't have emotion. This will not work much longer because you will find that what you pride yourself on will bring about your destruction.

You may feel as if you have worked things through with your parents. It would be more accurate to say that you have had as much vision as has been possible at a given time. When you experience some sort of bodywork or crystal work, or you create any kind of movement to higher ground, you get a bigger picture.

Information is stored and written in stone. Information is

also stored and written in bone. That is why it is important to work with the skeletal structure, because it houses much of your experience in this lifetime. Let things come out, and do not chastise yourself because you thought you were finished with certain events. Say, "This is wonderful! There is more here. I love it!" Use the experience as if you are discovering a gold mine— as if you are discovering that you are a newly birthed, wealthy person.

All you go through is what *you* decide you have to go through. You don't know how much you are clearing. You are opening avenues of consciousness for the planet, not just for yourselves. The good thing is that what you are clearing now is the easier stuff. Some of the far-out bizarre stuff will come later when you will be so blasé about it that it won't make any difference. Everything happens in its own time.

The mutation occurring is the evolution or plugging-in of internal data to external data. The clearing occurring is the accessing of all the emotional bodies you have been frightened of using. You need to access your emotional body in order to understand your spiritual body. As we have said, the mental body and the physical body go hand in hand, while the emotional body and the spiritual body go hand in hand. Because the spiritual body is nonphysical and you are locked in the physical realm, you must access the whole realm of the nonphysical through your emotions.

Human beings tend to love their dramas so much that they can get lost in the process of processing. Processing can become a way of life. This is not useful. It is not "cool" to always be processing and saying to people, "Don't call me, I'm processing. I'm deep in my stuff. I can't figure it out." Yes, your personal dramas need to be examined. Yes, your personal dramas are a banquet of nourishment for yourself. But, eat the food and get on with life and make yourself another banquet. Quit holding onto these gems of your past and being so frightened that if you resolve these issues you will never have anything else exciting come up again in your lives. It is good to put processing in perspective.

The human body is evolving and changing. It may believe that it needs a certain nutritional combination because this is what you have been taught. Ideally at this point, however, you will forget what you have been taught. You will listen to your body and let your body tell you what it wants. We would guess that many of you in the last year have changed the things you want to eat. You no longer feel comfortable eating what you used to eat because the vibration within certain food is so intense that it is not compatible with you. In the meat industry as you know it, the cattle, pigs, and chickens are not fed food. They live in small compartments, and many of them do not see the light of day. Many of them defecate on top of one another because they live in layers of small metal boxes. This is how they are raised. They are fed steroids and antibiotics—things other than food. They are not raised with love. When they are taken to slaughter, they are also not killed with love. So you are ingesting this vibration.

Remember that all things exist as a vibration. Animals were put upon the planet to be companions for you, to live on the land, and to feed you and shelter you if necessary. This was to be done with love. If you live on a farm and raise your own chickens and pigs, and if you feed them food, and if, when it comes time to bring them to slaughter, you do it with compassion and love, then it is fine. You give quality of life to the animals, and then the animals in turn recycle themselves to give you love and quality of life. That is the ideal. That was the reality for a long time upon this planet. It is not the reality any longer. Be aware of the vibration within things.

Let your body speak what it wants. Let yourself be willing to change, because your body, as it attempts to raise its vibration and build a light body, will move away from certain foods. Intend that you wish to change your diet and then intend that things come to you. We emphasize over and over again that you are much more than physical beings. You exist in many realities, and you have a multitude of guides. So each of you needs to become more clear in your intentions. What do you want? State, "I want to evolve. I want to change my diet. I wish to have a greater sense of intuition." Be clear about what you intend. The words *I intend* have tremendous power.

True health would consist of twelve completely mutated and evolved helixes inside the body, which would activate full brain capacity. It will take a while for the twelve helixes to be completely activated, though they can begin to be plugged in. Some of you have experienced them as plugged in, yet not activated. When they are in activation, the full brain is in operation and you are geniuses. You know everything, you are telepathic, and you are able to do anything because you are the host of the Living Library. You have the card that allows you to access any kind of information stored all over this planet.

If you could aspire to anything, we would ask you to become impeccable Keepers of Frequency. Keep inside yourself knowledge and information of the highest order, an order of unlimited being. Make that frequency, simply by living it, available to all around you by walking your streets, shopping in your stores, and simply resting on your pillows in the evening and knowing who you are.

There will come a time when you will no longer need to seek information outside of yourselves. At this time, we and others like us come to trigger you, to round you up, to gather you together, and to put you into clusters so that you can reflect off each other and electromagnetically charge each other. When we work with you, we create sparks of light that allow openings. As these openings occur within you, you vibrate at such a rate that you affect everyone around you. Whenever something clicks with one of you, you send out a frequency of recognition and other people pick it up. That is how the group mind grows. It occurs without you rationally understanding it or specifically having a picture or a realization of it because it happens electromagnetically within the body. You create the raising of energy according to how much you are able to handle.

Individuals must trigger themselves into multidimensionality. Part of the self makes a decision and says, "Alright, I wish to go into this multidimensional experience. What do I want to do?" The desire must come first. The desire is a realization that puts you in the moment. Then you must decide what you are going to do with this desire. You might forget it tomorrow. In order to structure this desire and demonstrate that you are really serious about it, participate in events, actions, rituals, and ceremonies that demonstrate your commitment. Then you can proceed to structure your life in such a way as to send the signal that this is what you mean. This can be like living and walking prayer. Churches teach people to pray and beg certain lords for things that they want or for forgiveness. We are suggesting a living prayer, a process by which every moment in the day has meaning and leads you because of the way you are acting and your focus on what you are praying for.

Living prayer involves having a very conscious intention about the objects in your environment: having an altar, having sacred things, and having nothing in your reality that does not have meaning for you. We know that suggesting you have nothing in your reality that has no meaning sends an earthquake through some of you. But how many of you are putting up with things you don't want in your life, whether it is the coat you have been wearing for the last fifteen years that has a few moth holes under the arm or the partner you have been carting around for thirty-five years who has more than a few moth holes? It is a challenge to get rid of everything in your life that does not have meaning for you, yet this is essential.

Putting an altar together is a great overlay for activating ritual. Ritual stirs up cellular memory and reminds you of ancient teachings that are stored inside you. It puts these teachings into your active memory. Ritual puts you in the now and takes you from one expanding now to another by honoring aspects of Mother Earth that have personal significance. You create personal significance for yourself. All things first come into being because someone decided to energize them. Anything can be energized. It comes down to the power of the individual mind to activate the will and use it to restructure reality.

There is no one on the Earth plane at this time who is not impulsed toward evolving. No one without this impulse would have come here. All the portals that were opened and the blueprints that were laid out for this time were conditioned to work toward self-motivating, self-accelerating, rapid evolution. This book itself is a process and a trigger. The keys are hidden within this book. We encourage you to act on the impulses that are whispering in your ear saying, "You are part of this Family of Light, and Earth is a Living Library." We will entice you and assist you by saying that there are many rewards. Even though we will never guarantee that the challenges will stop, there is a stance of mastery that you will achieve.

Learn to read the symbols and follow the impulses to their highest conclusion. Being multidimensional means opening the channels and turning the dials to the various frequencies, and then receiving the transmissions or knowings.

There are not enough words in the present vocabulary or dictionary of expression to convey the feelings of the nonphysical realm. The Spirit we speak of encompasses many ideas. It basically refers to that which is not physical or not within third-dimensional viewing.

You can liken this enticement or leap to bounding on a trampoline and going for one gigantic jump, after which you never touch the trampoline again. You bound and bound and then go for that gold that sends you into the realm of Spirit. This is not to say that you are lost or destroyed or that your molecules are disseminated. It is simply the vault that all of the ancient shamans on Earth practiced and maintained as a potentiality— a way of linking intelligent forms and assisting the evolving human species.

Multidimensionality to us is a way of life. We realize that part of our challenge as teachers is to transduce our way of life into systems that are evolving. To put you at rest, however, unless you check out of the planet, this is a process you are heading toward, though how you encounter it is up to you.

We want you to be able to go to the edge of a cliff, step off it, and stand in the air next to the cliff edge. We want you to be out there. We want you to recognize the heretic inside of you: the part that knows and is going to break this reality wide open and establish a whole new paradigm of consciousness. This is not going to be done by one world leader; it is going to be done by the masses, because the masses are ready for it.

At this time, the Guardians of Light are on this planet in the millions. All you need to do is evolve yourselves. Your work at this time is very intensely involved with the self, the physical vehicle that you presently occupy. It is the self that allows you to play this game at this time. Love it, honor it, cherish it, take good care of it, speak very well of it, and intend that it perform at optimum capacity. That is all you need do to be open to connect with your Family of Light. Then be prepared to find out who light has met, who light is going to introduce you to, and who light, indeed, *are*.

Love is what you experience when you go beyond light. You need light, which is information, to access this love. Without the informational frequency, the love frequency is misunderstood. When the love frequency comes first, without the light frequency, you think that love is outside of yourself rather than understanding that *it is you*. Then you do what people on the planet have done for eons: you worship and deify everything and think that love is *out there* rather than *in here*. We have decided to come onto this planet and operate with light first by informing you, strengthening you, and firing your blueprints according to information.

Now that you have become informed, and you understand what you are up against during the multidimensional light infusion with your identity, you will begin to experience the love frequency that will allow you to extend love to other versions of your multidimensional self and create a massive healing of consciousness on many levels. The experiences you will have in these realms of activity can be very powerful. They will alter you tremendously, and you will walk around with a smile from ear to ear so that others will wonder what you have been up to. You will carry yourself this way because you will be in a vibration of ecstasy. You will be in a vibration of connectedness, and everyone and everything you draw to yourself will be a part of that vibration. Anything that does not resonate with this frequency will not even be able to get near you. In actuality, when you resonate with the higher frequencies, anything that is not in those frequencies will not even *see* you.

When you operate in the frequency of information coupled with creation and love, you will be put to work spreading that frequency—not by doing it for others, but by allowing others to feel your frequency when they come in contact with you.

You all are invaluable, you know. Those of you who master these things, and there is no reason why all of you cannot, will be in very high demand one of these days. You will be looked upon as superhuman. However, it is not for you to separate yourself from the population. It is your place to teach the population and show them how they can do the same thing. Frequencies are to be given and shared freely so that everyone can discover what they can do for themselves. This is how this planet is going to evolve.

TWENTY-TWO

The Galactic Tidal Wave of Light

Awareness is awakening within the masses on this planet. The sum total of events as they quicken and unfold is seeping its way into everyone's reality. These events are orchestrated and designed to bring you collectively, as a species, to this new octave of light expression. This infusion from the galactic tidal wave of light comes from the future through portals you open on this Earth plane as you follow and weave yourself through the journey and story we have shared with you. The masses are awakening. You see them around you and feel the rumblings of consciousness, the internal Earth changes, which will truly mark the rites of passage for all of humanity.

We have, with the greatest assistance from our teachers, presented to this planet information that we feel can harmonize our purposes and pool our energies. We feel that we have given to this planet at this time a succinct message of inspiration—a message that holds waves of truth. It is a message to tickle—a message to entice and call forward that part of the self that has been hidden away and lying dormant. We feel that the material we have been sharing through this book is to awaken within you what you know. It is to bring you to an understanding of the different versions of your reality's illusion as it is sold to you and to an understanding of what your part in all of this is or can be.

We have stimulated each and every one of you with our

thought-provoking messages. It has been our intention to move each one of you and stir you from some place, not to make you uncomfortable. You may make yourselves uncomfortable; we encourage you to find comfort. We also encourage you to climb a few mountain ranges of consciousness within yourself: to go to new places of comfort and to find those valleys of eternal youth, eternal vitality, and ongoing expression of creativity. There you will find new vistas of consciousness and a galactic wave of light from the future.

It is our intention in delivering this final message in chapter 22, the final chapter, to use the vibration of the number 22, a master number. This number is associated with imprinting and delivering into this version of physical reality a master teaching—a message that involves an encoding. The message is not simply in the way the words are strung together: there are layers of information hidden within the method and unfoldment of this book. Ideas are presented, conflicts arise, solutions are suggested, and inspiration weaves its way through, turning you always to that final commitment to inspire yourself.

We feel that you will benefit from this orchestration that we have been influencing behind the scenes. There is a process of understanding that this book represents. Where it seems that there has been chaos and confusion, and where it seems as if things have been scrambled, that scrambling has created its own order. This order is being summed up in this final delivery under the stamp of 22.

In this final message, we speak into the soul and heart of every one of you. We ask you to hear the call, to recognize it, and to step forward as a member of the Family of Light. Have the courage in all the days you walk this planet to live that light and share it with all you encounter. This does not mean to preach or sell that light. It means to live the light you know you are, to discover in the simplicity of your being the purpose of your existence, to blossom with it, and to reseed this place that is Planet Earth in its deepest time of transition.

The process of moving into this higher octave of understanding—this blending of dimensions and creation of new territory—will lead everyone through greater understanding of death. Your light will be needed. Your light represents what you know. This book has many ways, through designs and codes that you have been unable to recognize, to remind you in these final pages that you know everything we speak of and that it is inside of you. It is time for you to share the discoveries and miracles of operating the physical vehicle in these times of change and transition that involve the death of the world as you know it. When there is a death, there is always a rebirth; something dies and something new is born.

As this planet moves closer to these days of great change, each of you will be called upon to stand as pillars of light. You will show the way in times when people are desperate because the old ways are no longer solutions—they no longer fit and no longer apply. We have intimated or suggested in this book that light brings about much of this chaos on the planet. So, during these times, your gifts will be needed. You cannot run and hide, because you are needed to weave through the communities to bring alternative ways of being. You are needed to share your belief in creating reality through your thoughts and to show others how this works by healing and creating new ideals of civilization and cooperation.

As the days begin to unfold, they will reveal the ancient prophecies as they are coming alive. These ancient prophecies will be much more colorful and have their own versions of themselves as they teach this planet its greatest lessons.

As you evolve, you carry what you know forward, and you share it and live it. You become a greater vessel or greater expression of light. Through this process, you will find that over the next few years you will be catapulted beyond the speed of light with what you will know. The abilities and talents and information that will come to you are simply inside of you.

We will remind you that there is a galactic tidal wave of light from the future coming toward your planet and that this intersection will be felt throughout the masses in the year 1993. It will be as if the entire planet has a unilateral raise in consciousness. This wave has to be gigantic to affect all of the masses who are locked in frequency control. It is you, the Family of Light, who are here in the millions making room in your bodies for this galactic tidal wave, who will allow this infusion of the first layer of the light body to be held by all of the masses.

The light body is the body that holds the complete mutation of the species. It will be able to juggle realities through the shifting of consciousness by intent from one view to another, like turning the stations on a television. The light body will hold all of this encoded data and be able to translate it at will. It will communicate innerdimensionally and interdimensionally.

Remember, matter is simply light that is trapped. As you build your light body, you are allowing a reorganization of the molecular structure—a loosening of your grip upon a certain aspect of materialism so that your spiritual understanding can be more in tune with your day-to-day life. The building of the light body is the allowing of less trapped matter to manifest and allow light, which is freer in expression and in seeking its own source, to become who you are so that you are not so solid.

As you raise your vibratory rates, you become your light body. You will see the change in your body literally. Your body will become more vital, more youthful, more nourished in its own being, and definitely the processor of a multitude of information. It will become a super being. The building of the light body involves becoming a super being.

Extending the longevity of the cellular body through rejuvenation and extension of cellular life is coming back into fashion. This is part of building the light body—a body that is not so dense, that does not self-destruct, that self-generates, and that self-replenishes. That is what you are all striving for. You would be your light body, and you would feel it, if your logical mind were not so worried about whether it is possible; society is not telling you it is possible.

We cannot emphasize enough to you that you must stop listening to society. This is going to be the hardest task for you to do and the biggest break for you to make. You have the societal self and the spiritual self, and you must decide which one is sacred. Which one is your source of authority? Let your intuitive self become your authority. Allow your intuitive self to be the standard bearer of your experience, which is experience no one else is going to validate. Your experience springs from the assignment that you are knowing, and not necessarily remembering, you are on.

If you approach all that you know with the stance that there is divine order and divine purpose, without your ego aspect comprehending it all the time, you will move rapidly through realities. There will be many different ways this galactic tidal wave of light will be experienced. Definitely it will catapult everyone into some exaggerated version of their greatest opportunity. That, of course, is each person's choice.

Our final words include a thank-you to all of you who recognize the light source that is a part of your identity and that moves you to read this book and follow the silent whispers that echo down the golden spirals through the corridors of your own being. We honor you, we recognize you, and we are here to assist you. We are all here as the Family of Light to bring that choice and that freedom to evolve back onto this planet— to bring it to this place where it will shine as a portion of the Living Library, a new star, a new light on the horizons of many sentient worlds.

We wait in the future for your past to intersect our present and catapult all of existence to a new octave, the highest octave of being. It is our great pleasure to have your assistance in this process.

ABOUT THE AUTHOR

The Pleiadians are a collective of extraterrestrials from the star system the Pleiades. They have been speaking through Barbara Marciniak since May 18, 1988; they say they were conceived on Harmonic Convergence and birthed in Athens, Greece, nine months later. The Pleiadian collective was originally composed of seventy-five to one hundred entities. Now they often refer to themselves as Pleiadians Plus, indicating a joining of forces with other extraterrestrials.

The Pleiadian teachings can be likened to those of shamanism, that ancient body of consciousness that has served as intermediary between the realms of the physical and the spiritual, leading people to self-discovery in the worlds of paradox, paradigm shifting, and spirituality.

Barbara Marciniak is an internationally known trance channel from North Carolina. She began channeling in May of 1988 in Athens, Greece, at the conclusion of a three-week journey through ancient Egypt and Greece. On this trip, Barbara was impulsed to reexperience specific temples and power sites in this lifetime—the Great Pyramid at Giza, the temples along the Nile, the Acropolis in Athens, and Delphi.

Since that time, Barbara has conducted class sessions and workshops throughout the United States and has facilitated tours to sacred power sites such as Peru, Mexico, Egypt, Greece, Bali, and Australia. She feels that the sites themselves are connections to energy vortexes that hold knowledge of the higher mind, the higher idea that the Earth is presently seeking to re-create.

Barbara feels that her experience with the Pleiadians has been a gift of priceless value. Her work has connected her with opportunities for personal, global, and cosmic transformation, and for this she holds tremendous gratitude.